HIT & RUN:

NANCY & JJ

Roxanne Rose1

Dedication

This book is dedicated to the only being that unconditionally loves me.

Roxanne

Table of Contents

Chapter One:
The Body

Cody wouldn't stop barking. Nancy had let him out to do his business for the last time that night. He always came right home after he finished. Tonight, though he wouldn't come when she called him and he kept barking. I hope he hasn't found a porcupine she thought as she pulled on her jacket to go get him.

A rush of disbelief and horror crashed into her, momentarily paralyzing her thoughts. Linda, her former ICU colleague, lay broken and barely clinging to life.

Nancy's training kicked in, overriding the shock. "Hang on," she whispered, her voice thick. She forced herself to move, to act. She had no idea how long Linda had been out here, exposed to the night's chill.

Pushing to her feet, she spun and sprinted back toward the house. "Debbie!" she shouted, her voice ragged. "Call an ambulance—now!"

Without waiting for a response, she grabbed a blanket from the couch, her hands fumbling in her urgency. "Come with me," she urged Debbie, yanking open the door.

Every second mattered. Every breath Linda took was slipping away. And Nancy refused to let her go without a fight.

Debbie ran after her mother. Nancy covered Linda with the blanket but didn't move her because she was unsure of her injuries. She spoke to her but there was no response.

"I'm going to support her head, neck and shoulders," Nancy said. "You try to turn her very slightly on her side so she can breathe better." Debbie did as asked. Linda remained unresponsive, but her breathing seemed a little improved.

"What do we do now?" Debbie asked.

"We wait for the ambulance and protect her as best we can."

The wait for the ambulance felt like an eternity, each passing minute stretching into what seemed like an hour. Nancy stood frozen in place, her mind racing through a thousand thoughts, unable to focus on any one of them for long enough to make sense of what was happening.

When the ambulance finally arrived, the EMTs moved with practiced efficiency, assessing Linda's condition in what felt like mere seconds. They slipped a cervical collar around Linda's neck with expert hands, their calm professionalism offering a small comfort in the chaos.

With delicate precision, they positioned a backboard under her, gently rolling her body while ensuring that her head, neck, and back were fully supported. Nancy's heart twisted at the sight, but she stayed still, watching in silence as they carefully lifted Linda onto the backboard and transferred her onto a stretcher.

The driver's voice was steady as he notified the local medical center of the incoming patient. One of the EMTs climbed into the back of the ambulance, already checking Linda's vital signs, the sound of scissors snipping through fabric filling the air as he cut away the front of Linda's hoodie and t-shirt. He quickly hooked her up to a cardiac monitor, his movements swift and efficient.

The second EMT, a woman with a calm demeanor, started an IV, her eyes focused on the task at hand.

Nancy and Debbie stood there, watching as the EMTs worked in unison, their quiet professionalism doing little to soothe the fear gnawing at Nancy's insides. The sound of the ambulance doors slamming shut echoed in the still night air, and Nancy felt a shudder run through her.

With the flick of a switch, the ambulance's lights flashed to life, and the sirens wailed as the driver slammed the gas pedal, heading toward the medical center. Nancy's eyes followed them until the vehicle disappeared into the distance, her stomach twisting into a knot.

"Please let her make it," Nancy whispered to herself, her voice barely audible as she stood frozen, rooted to the spot, unable to move.

We need to call Linda's mother," Nancy said, her voice tight with urgency. She turned to Debbie, who nodded, her face pale under the porch light.

As they made their way back to the house, Nancy reached down and ran her fingers through Cody's fur. "Good boy," she murmured, her voice shaky. If not for him… she swallowed hard, unable to finish the thought.

Inside, she hurried to the kitchen, her hands fumbling as she flipped through an old notepad until she found Barbara's number. The numbers blurred for a moment, and she exhaled sharply, forcing herself to focus.

Her fingers trembled as she punched in the digits, each beep of the dial tone stretching the knots in her stomach tighter. How could she even begin to say this?

She pressed the phone to her ear, inhaling sharply as it rang. Please pick up. Please let me find the right words.

When Barbara answered the phone, Linda identified herself. "What do you want?" Barbara asked nastily based on the problems Linda and Nancy had had in the past.

"Barbara, I have some bad news," she said. She continued before Barbara could interrupt. "Linda was found by my dog on the side of the road about a quarter of a mile from my house. I think she may have been hit by a car. She didn't respond when I spoke to her, but she had a pulse and was breathing. I ran home and called an ambulance. She is on her way to the medical center right now."

There was a long silence. Then Barbara said, "Oh my God I don't know what to do. Tom has my car and his truck is at the shop. I don't know how to get a hold of him. I think he was out drinking with his buddies."

"Would you like me to pick you up and take you to the medical center?"

"I don't know what to do." Barbara paused. "I guess that would be best. I don't know when Tom will be home. But I need to check that Brenda is home to watch Linda's kids."

"We can stop there on the way if you like."

"Okay."

"I'll pick you up right now."

"Thank you," Barbara said and hung up.

Debra grabbed her car keys. "You watch the kids Debbie. I don't know when I'll be home." She gave Cody a treat, told him what a good dog he was again and left to pick up Barbara.

Barbara was standing outside waiting for her when she arrived at her house. Barbara walked over to the car, looking at it strangely before she got in.

"What happened to your car she asked?"

"I hit a deer last week and it broke the cover of my right light and dented the bumper. I am saving up to get it fixed but it drives fine and the lights work. When I have some money, I'll get it fixed. My insurance will pay some but I have $500 deductible. It might be cheaper to fix it myself so my insurance doesn't go up."

They drove to Linda's house and Barbara went in to check on the children. Brenda had just gotten home from a date with her boyfriend, Steve. Barbara told Brenda she needed to watch the children because her mother had been hit by a car and was at the medical center. All of the children had lots of questions, but Brenda looked horrified.

Barbara said, "I don't know anything except she was hit by a car and was taken by ambulance to the medical center. I will call you as soon as I know anything, but I need to go now. Linda is driving me there."

Barbara left the house amid questions and crying. She got back into Linda's car and they drove off.

Linda asked, "Is Brenda there to watch the kids?"

Barbara replied, "Yes. The kids were naturally upset and had a million questions, but I told them I would call as soon as I knew anything. They were all crying as I left. Brenda seemed to be in shock and didn't say anything. I thought that was a little strange."

"I notice you got rid of your van. You might not have had as much damage with the van," Barbara said.

"A patient of mine went to a nursing home and his wife offered me his car at a great price. It was a Chevy SUV like yours. I figured your husband being in the business would know a good car, so I bought it and sold the van. Also, it has 4-wheel drive, which is great in the winter and is much better on gas."

They drove the rest of the way in silence. When they arrived, Nancy walked into the medical center with Barbara.

Chapter Two:
The Medical Center

At the admission desk, they inquired about Linda. Shortly a nurse with a tired but kind expression appeared. Her name tag read Miriam Carter. She looked up at them - "How may I be of help please?"

"We're here to see Linda. She was rushed in here following a road traffic accident," Barbara answered, forcing the words out.

"Linda Daniels," Nancy added urgently.

"Yes, she's in surgery right now," the nurse replied, flipping through the chart she held dearly like a priest holds his holy book. "Are you family?"

"I'm her friend," Nancy answered. She gestured toward Barbara. "This is her mother, Mrs. Barbara Berry." "He took my car," Barbara muttered under her breath. "If I had it, I would've been here sooner."

Nancy glanced over at her, softening her tone. "You're here now, Barbara. That's the most important thing."

Miriam's expression softened. She felt really sad for them, especially Barbara. No mother should have to hear what she's about to tell her regarding the daughter's injuries. "I'm so sorry. Please, sit down, and I'll explain her condition."

Barbara sank into the nearest chair, her hands trembling in her lap. Nancy sat beside her, rubbing her back gently as Miriam pulled up a stool and began to explain.

"Linda was brought in unconscious with multiple critical injuries," Miriam began, her voice steady but laced with gravity. "She sustained a severe head injury, including an intracerebral hemorrhage—bleeding in the brain. The neurosurgeons are in surgery now, working to relieve the pressure and stop the bleeding."

She paused, giving them a moment to absorb the weight of her words, careful not to overwhelm them with too much at once.

Barbara let out a soft, strangled gasp, her hands flying to her mouth. Her eyes shimmered with unshed tears, terror widening them as though she couldn't fully process what she'd just heard.

Nancy, her own heart heavy yet her mind sharpening with focus, reached over and gave Barbara's hand a firm, reassuring squeeze.

Miriam continued gently but firmly. "There's also a basal skull fracture. Fortunately, the CT scan shows it's not too severe, but we're monitoring her closely." She exhaled slightly, softening her tone. "For now, she'll remain under sedation."

The sterile hum of the hospital filled the silence that followed, each second stretching unbearably as the weight of the unknown pressed down on them.

Miriam hesitated, choosing her words carefully. "There's a chance Nancy will make it, but of course, these types of conditions can be tricky. The surgery will help stabilize her, but with head trauma, there's always some uncertainty. The next 24 to 48 hours will be critical and it will determine her overall outcome."

Barbara squeezed her eyes shut, fighting back tears.

Nancy asked, her tone professional but strained, "Is there any other injury apart from the cerebral hemorrhage?"

Miriam pressed on gently. "Linda fractured her right femur and also has three fractured ribs on the left side which caused bruising to her lungs. The pulmonologist inserted a chest tube and also placed her on a ventilator to support her breathing until her lungs recovered."

Barbara shook her head, tears rolling freely down her face, overwhelmed by the list of injuries. "She was just walking... and now this."

Miriam's voice softened. "So sorry about how you feel, Mrs. Berry. We're doing everything we can. Even though it might be a long road to recovery, we'll do our best to return your daughter back to you, Mrs. Berry."

Nancy's jaw clenched. Whoever had done this had not only broken Linda's body but had left her to die. And now, Nancy had to hold it together - for her friend and for Barbara.

Chapter Three:
Barbara is Missing

Tom Berry, drunk as he was, knew he had hit something—or someone. His pulse pounded against his skull as he pulled his wife's car into the garage, the harsh overhead light exposing the damage like a guilty wound. The front right fender was crumpled, the headlight smashed, the bumper hanging loose.

His hands trembled slightly as he worked, stripping away the damaged parts and stacking them in the corner. He threw a drop cloth over them, as if that could erase what had happened. Then, with a deep breath, he locked the garage and climbed into his truck, driving home at a crawl, his mind replaying the impact over and over.

By the time he pulled into the driveway, exhaustion settled over him like a heavy fog. He had sobered up a little, but his body ached with the weight of the night. Still, now that he was home, what harm could one more beer do?

He cracked it open, flicked on the TV, and sank into the couch, the alcohol numbing his nerves. Before he knew it, sleep pulled him under.

Morning light streamed through the blinds when he jolted awake, his mouth dry, his body stiff. Something felt... off. No smell of coffee. No clatter of dishes. No sound of his wife moving about the kitchen.

Frowning, he glanced at his watch—**9 a.m.** She always got up at seven to make his breakfast.

His stomach tightened. **Why was the house so quiet?**

Heart hammering, he pushed himself up and headed upstairs to check on her.

When he opened the bedroom door, he was greeted by a neatly made empty bed. His wife was nowhere around. He called her name as he walked around the house, but there was no response and he couldn't find her anywhere. Linda must have gotten her, he thought. She's probably mad that I stayed out so late last night and fell asleep on the couch.

He called Linda's house and Brenda answered. She sounded like she was crying. "Is your grandmother there?" he asked.

"No," she sobbed.

"What's the matter?"

"Mom is in the medical center. Nancy took Grandma there last night."

"Why is Linda in the medical center?"

"She got hit by a car, had surgery, went to ICU and is in a coma."

"I got home last night and thought your grandmother was in bed. I watched some TV and fell asleep on the couch. When I woke up this morning, I found she was gone and couldn't figure it out. I am going to head for the medical center right now. Are you and the kids alright?".

"We're worried and aren't going to school today, but we are otherwise ok. Call us to let us know more about her condition."

"I will."

Tom pulled on a jacket, went out to get in his truck and headed to the medical center. He drove carefully trying to remember the night before. He had damaged his wife's car. He remembered swerving to avoid the oncoming car and hitting something or someone. Did he hit his own daughter he wondered? The thought horrified him and he put it out of his mind as best he could.

When he arrived at the medical center he hurried into registration.

"I am here to see Linda Daniels," he said.

"She is in ICU. Are you a relative?" the registration clerk asked.

"I'm her father."

"Go straight down the hallway, it's the second door on the left. Push the red button and someone will let you in," she directed.

He did as she said and waited for someone to open the door. Eventually, a nurse in scrubs opened the door.

"How may I help you?" she asked.

"I'm Linda Williams' father. Can I see her?" he asked.

"Yes, your wife is with her now," she said, smelling the stench of old alcohol on his breath.

She led him to a room with glass doors and a curtain pulled to provide privacy for the patient. As he walked around the curtain, he saw his wife sitting in a chair next to the bed holding Linda's hand.

Linda's eyes were closed and she had tubes coming out of her nose, mouth arms and a bag hanging with yellow fluid that appeared to be urine. She was hooked to a cardiac monitor with lines of different colors squiggling across the screen. There were bandages on her head and left hand and arm.

His wife stood up and hugged him with tears in her eyes.

"Where were you last night?" she asked.

"I was out with the boys," he replied. Then on the way home, I hit a deer with your car, so I took it to the garage to get it fixed. I took my truck home and assumed you were in bed. I turned on the TV and fell asleep on the couch. When I woke up this morning and couldn't find you, I called Linda. Brenda answered and told me you were at the medical center and Linda had been hit by a car. I got here as soon as I knew."

"Nancy drove me here and has been here all night. She's in the waiting room. I will tell her she can go home now and get some sleep."

Chapter Four:
Doctors

Barbara exhaled slowly. "The doctors say she's lucky to be alive. They've done everything they can for now, but…" She trailed off, looking down at her hands. "It's too early to know what the long-term damage will be."

Tom wiped a hand over his face, cursing himself for sleeping soundly while his daughter fought for her life. "I should have been here sooner."

Barbara gave him a weary look. "What matters is that you're here now. Why don't you sit with her for a bit? I'll encourage Nancy to go home and get some rest."

She walked to the waiting room where Nancy was quietly sitting, with her head resting on the wall. She looked up as Barbara approached.

"Nancy," Barbara said gently, "you've done so much already. Why don't you go home, get some rest, and come back later? We'll be here with her."

Nancy hesitated, reluctant to leave her friend in such a fragile state, but the exhaustion weighed heavily on her. She knew she wasn't much help in this condition. She had called her kids last night and again this morning, but she needed to get home to make sure they had gotten on the buses for school.

"All right," Nancy whispered, squeezing Barbara's hand. "But call me if anything changes."

Barbara gave her a grateful smile. "I will."

Nancy stood, stretched, the weight of the last 24 hours followed her out the door.

. .
.

Shortly after Nancy left, the steady rhythm of beeping monitors was interrupted by the quiet shuffle of footsteps. A trio of doctors entered Linda's room, their white coats swaying as they moved with practiced efficiency. Dr. Patel, the neurosurgeon, led the way, flanked by Dr. Roberts, the orthopedic surgeon, and Dr. Faulkner, the pulmonologist. They murmured among themselves, flipping through charts, their expressions serious but composed.

Tom and Barbara stood in the corner, their eyes heavy with exhaustion. Barbara clutched her hands together, the weight of the last 24 hours pressing down on her, deepening the lines on her face. She barely recognized the reflection she had glimpsed in the mirror that morning—worn, aged, and utterly drained.

Dr. Patel, his dark eyes warm with reassurance, offered a small smile as he stepped closer. He was young, confident, and had the kind of effortless charm that belonged on a movie screen rather than a hospital ward.

"Good morning, Mr. and Mrs. Berry," he said gently, his voice calm but authoritative. "I know this has been an overwhelming time for you both, but my colleagues and I wanted to give you an update on Linda's condition."

He pointed toward the chart. "The surgery went well, and we were able to stop the bleeding in her brain. The swelling has gone down, too, which is a good sign. We've kept her sedated to give her brain time to heal."

Barbara clutched Tom's arm tightly. "Will she wake up soon? When can I talk to her today?"

Dr. Patel nodded slowly. "We'll begin reducing the sedation slowly. Once she's completely off sedation, she will wake up at her own time."

Barbara, looking pale and as if she'd aged another 10 years in the past 5 minutes, asked about the broken leg in a low, fearful voice.

Dr. Roberts, the orthopedic surgeon, looked at her after surveying the notes he was holding. "We'll need to schedule surgery to repair her femur in the coming days. Right now, our main concern is stabilizing her so she can safely undergo the procedure."

Barbara swallowed hard and asked, "And the ribs?"

Dr. Faulkner, the pulmonologist, spoke calmly. "Her ribs are healing on their own, but we'll continue monitoring her lungs for any signs of complications. She's still on the ventilator, but once she's stable, we'll try to wean her off it."

Dr. Patel folded his arms, his expression serious but reassuring. "I won't sugarcoat things… Linda has a long road to recovery ahead of her. She's alive, and that's a blessing, but we can't predict the extent of her impairments just yet.

Brain injuries are complicated. Some people recover fully, while others may have lingering effects."

Tom cleared his throat, his voice hoarse. "But you're certain she'll wake up from this, right?"

The doctors exchanged glances, and Dr. Patel gave a small, encouraging nod. "Yes, we believe she will survive. She's shown signs of resilience. However, the degree of recovery is uncertain. Whether it's mental, physical, or emotional recovery. It will depend on how her brain heals in the coming weeks."

Barbara took a shaky breath, feeling half relieved and half terrified. "So, she's not out of the woods yet." Tears, which never desert her at times of need, started rolling down her cheeks.

"No," Dr. Patel replied, "but she's making progress, and that's what we focus on for now."

"We'll do our best to get your daughter as close to full recovery as possible. She's in good hands." Dr Roberts added.

Barbara and Tim nodded numbly, grateful for the doctors' careful explanations even though they were still overwhelmed by the uncertainty.

As the doctors finished their rounds and left, Barbara sank into the chair beside Linda's bed, brushing a strand of hair from her daughter's bruised forehead. "She's going to pull through," Barbara whispered, more to herself than anyone else. Tim stood behind her, silent.

Together, they watched their daughter breathe. Each rise and fall of her chest served as a reminder that she was still with them, even if the road ahead was unknown.

Chapter Five:
The Investigation Begins

While Linda lay in the medical center, caught between life and death, the police were alerted to the accident. Responding swiftly, officers arrived at the scene, their radios crackling in the crisp morning air. The EMT who had found Linda led them to the spot, his face still pale from the sight of her broken body. The area was cordoned off, yellow tape flapping in the breeze as if whispering warnings to the world—something terrible had happened here.

At first light, Detective Jason and a forensic analyst stepped onto the scene, their boots crunching against the gravel. Jason exhaled slowly, taking in the eerie silence. No witnesses, no obvious answers—only the remnants of violence left behind. The forensic analyst moved methodically, documenting shards of shattered glass glinting in the morning sun, flecks of blue and silver paint clinging to the pavement, and dark stains of blood dried into the earth. Stray strands of hair clung to the gravel like silent cries for help. A few cigarette butts lay scattered nearby—maybe from the driver, maybe from a bystander. Tire tracks etched into the ground hinted at a sudden swerve, a moment of panic frozen in time.

Each piece of evidence was more than just an object; it was part of a story waiting to be uncovered. Jason watched as the team photographed, collected, and carefully sealed every fragment. Blood samples were rushed off for analysis. The broken glass and paint chips—silent witnesses to the impact—were sent to the State Police lab for identification. The tire tracks, blurred by ambulance wheels and bystanders' footsteps, were beyond saving, lost to the chaos of the night.

Jason ran a hand through his hair, a knot tightening in his chest. He'd seen scenes like this before, but they never got easier. Someone had left Linda here—left her to die. The evidence spoke in whispers, fragments of truth scattered in the dirt. It was his job to listen, to put the pieces together.

And somewhere out there, the driver was hoping he never would.

. .
.

While JJ was investigating, Nancy had driven home. She stopped at Linda's house on the way to check on her kids. Most of them were asleep in the living room, but Brenda was awake and looked agitated.

"How are you?" she asked.

"Upset, worried and I have a lot of questions," answered Brenda.

"I'll fill you in as best I can. Your mother has a head injury, which they think they have stabilized. She has a broken femur, that will be repaired when they think it is safe to do surgery. There are some broken ribs, so she has a chest tube and is on a ventilator to breathe for her. She has a lot of cuts and bruises. The doctors are optimistic at this stage, but her recovery will take a long time".

When can I see her?" Brenda asked.

"That's up to your grandparents, but now I need to go check on my children. Don't hesitate to call me if you need anything like food, other supplies or help with the children."

"Thank you," Brenda said, but she looked distraught.

Nancy hated to leave her, but she had her own children to check on. When she got home, the kitchen was a mess from breakfast. She was too tired to deal with that, having been up most of the night with an occasional nap in the waiting room. It appeared that at least the kids had gotten to school. She headed to bed and fell almost immediately into a deep sleep.

. .
.

The phone was ringing and she got up to answer it, afraid it might be one of her kids needing a ride home from school.

"Hello", said, expecting one of the kids to say Mom.

Surprisingly, it was Detective Jason, nicknamed (JJ). "Hi," he said. I understand you found Linda on the side of the road unconscious."

"Yes."

"Do you mind if I ask how?"

"I let my dog Cody out to pee. Shortly after, he started barking and wouldn't stop. He wouldn't come when I called him so I went to get him. When I found him, he was standing beside a body on the side of the road that was not moving."

"I immediately checked for a pulse. When I pulled back the hoodie the person was wearing, I saw that it was Linda. I checked her breathing and it was shallow. I went home, grabbed a blanket, asked Debbie to call an ambulance and to come help me."

"With me supporting her neck and shoulders, Debbie was able to turn her slightly so her breathing improved a bit. Then we stayed with her and waited for the ambulance. Once they arrived, we went home and called her mother," Nancy ended.

"Did you see any cars in the area?" he asked.

"No, it was late and there were no cars around," she replied.

"I will have some policemen canvass the area going house to house to see if anyone heard or saw anything unusual on the road last night. They might also find some car parts or other clues along the road."

"How is Linda doing?" JJ asked.

"I think in terms of your investigation it would be better if you talked to her doctors."

"That makes sense. Hey, how about a movie and dinner on Saturday?"

"I would love to, but let's see how things go with Linda. I feel sort of obligated to her family since I found her and it was close to my house. Give me a call on Friday, okay?"

"Sounds good."

. .
.

Nancy got up and one by one her kids returned home as she was preparing dinner.

"Why don't you all start your homework while I finish making dinner?"
How's Linda doing?" Debbie asked.

"She is stable for now, but still in a coma. I will probably go back for a while tonight to check on her and give her mother a break. I won't stay too late as I have to work tomorrow. My new job as Director of ICU starts next week. Then I will have more regular hours, but I will be working every day, Monday through Friday."

She finished preparing dinner and they all sat down to eat.

"How was school today? I see you all caught your buses."

"Boring," said Bob.

"We had a great basketball practice," replied Bill.

"I might as well tell you now as you'll probably find out. I skipped school today with Jennifer. I couldn't stop thinking about Linda lying on the side of the road and not talking," said Debbie.

"I understand, Debbie. Do you want to go tomorrow and talk to your counselor instead of going to classes?" asked Nancy.

"I don't know. Can I decide in the morning?"

"Yes, but you need to go to school one way or the other."

They finished dinner and Nancy told them to do their homework while she cleaned up the kitchen.

When she finished, she said, "I am going back to the medical center now. When I get back, I want your homework done and everyone in bed. I will come up to say goodnight and go to bed myself."

Chapter Six:
Evening Rounds

It's evening time and the sun was dipping below the horizon. The soft hum of fluorescent lights illuminated the ICU. Linda's nurse was encouraging Barbara to go home and get some sleep. "We will be monitoring Linda all day and there is nothing you can do here except exhaust yourself which won't help her," she said.

"The night nurse said even though she's in a coma she might be able to hear me talk to her. I don't want her to feel abandoned," Barbara replied.

Nancy paused at the threshold of Linda's hospital room, her fingers brushing against the doorframe. She inhaled deeply, steadying herself before stepping inside. The air was thick with antiseptic and the rhythmic beeping of monitors, a stark contrast to the warmth Linda had always radiated in life. Having spent the night in the waiting room, she hadn't actually seen Linda since she found her on the side of the road.

Linda lay still, her face almost unrecognizable beneath the pallor and the bruises darkening her temples. Wires and tubes trailed from her fragile frame, tethering her to the machines that now kept her stable. The sight sent a pang through Nancy's chest, a sharp reminder of how quickly life could shatter.

Barbara sat beside the bed, her hands folded tightly in her lap, her gaze locked on her daughter as though sheer willpower could bring her back. The exhaustion in her posture was unmistakable, the weight of helplessness etched in the lines of her face.

Tom slumped in the corner, his head tilted back, mouth slightly open. Asleep. Whether it was exhaustion or the remnants of alcohol dulling his senses, Nancy didn't know. She swallowed down her irritation. Now wasn't the time.

Silently, she pulled a chair closer to the bed, her eyes never leaving Linda's face.

Barbara stirred, pressing her fingers to her temples before turning to Nancy with a tired smile. "You're back." Her voice was raw, barely above a whisper.

Nancy nodded. "I'm here." She hesitated, then reached for Barbara's hand, giving it a gentle squeeze. "You should go home for a bit. Get some rest, take a shower, and eat something. The kids need you, too. I'm sure they're desperate for an update."

Barbara exhaled, her shoulders sagging. "I don't know if I can leave her."

"I know," Nancy said softly. "But you need to take care of yourself, too. I'll stay. She won't be alone."

Barbara's lips trembled, and for a moment, it looked like she might argue. Instead, she nodded, her grip tightening around Nancy's before letting go.

Nancy turned back to Linda, her fingers brushing against the cool skin of her hand. Come back to us, Linda. We're all waiting

Barbara went to the edge of the room and dragged Tom out of his slumber. As they left the room, Nancy heard the quiet swish of the door and the fading tap of their shoes down the hallway. Now it was just the two of them, Nancy and Linda.

Nancy sat in silence, watching the slow, mechanical rise and fall of Linda's chest as the ventilator pushed air into her lungs.

She leaned back in the chair, her fingers brushing lightly over the bed's side rail. Memories occupied her mind, pulling her back to the early years of their friendship. She and Linda had been inseparable once. They were two young women navigating the chaos of adulthood together. They had laughed until their sides hurt, shared their dreams over bottles of cheap wine, and supported each other through heartbreaks and career challenges.

But somewhere along the way, Linda had pulled them apart over the job she so desperately wanted. Nancy wasn't sure if things could ever return back to normalcy, but all she wanted now was for Linda to recover her health.

Nancy stared at Linda's pale face now, guilt gnawing at her. How could Linda have let their friendship slip away over a job? And now, with Linda lying unconscious and vulnerable, she wondered if they would ever get the chance to rekindle what they had lost.

"I'm sorry, Linda," Nancy whispered. Her voice was barely audible over the steady sound of the ventilator. "I should have supported you rather than competing with you."

She reached out and gently took Linda's hand, her thumb tracing slow circles over her friend's cold skin. "You're going to get through this. You have to."

Nancy squeezed her eyes shut, holding back tears. She had seen too many patients in situations like this before. Some made miraculous recoveries; others not so much. It is days like these that make her cherish ignorance. At least if she wasn't a healthcare practitioner herself, she would have been expecting a full recovery. But she refused to believe that Linda wouldn't wake up. She couldn't.

Her thoughts were interrupted by the soft knock on the door. Nancy looked up as the doctors entered for their evening rounds. Dr. Faulkner, the pulmonologist, led the group, followed by Dr. Patel, the neurosurgeon, and Dr. Roberts, the orthopedic surgeon. They greeted Nancy with brief nods as they gathered around Linda's bed, flipping through charts and reviewing the data on the monitors.

Dr. Faulkner leaned in, his brow furrowing slightly as he studied the ventilator settings and the numbers on the screen. Nancy sat up straighter, immediately sensing something had changed.

"Her respiratory rate is up," Dr. Faulkner murmured, glancing at his colleagues. "It was steady earlier, but now she's breathing faster, despite being on the ventilator."

Nancy's pulse quickened. "What does that mean?" she asked, her voice sharp with concern.

Dr. Faulkner straightened, folding his arms. "It could be a sign that her body is under stress. There might be a buildup of carbon dioxide, or she could be developing an issue with oxygen exchange in the lungs."

Nancy's mind raced through the possibilities. "Do you think it's an infection? Pneumonia?"

Dr. Faulkner gave a small nod. "It's possible. We'll need to check. I'm going to put in an A-line and do an arterial blood gas to see what's happening with her oxygen and carbon dioxide levels. We'll also use the A-line to take blood samples to do a full blood count. That should give us a clear picture if she's septic."

Nancy shifted in her seat, her heart pounding. She knew how critical ABG results could be in determining a patient's condition. If Linda's lungs were struggling, it could complicate her recovery even further.

"What other tests are you considering?" she asked, her professional instincts kicking in despite the personal nature of the situation.

Dr. Faulkner exchanged a glance with the other doctors. Deciding on how much detail to give out.

"We'll also do a chest X-ray to look for any signs of fluid buildup or infection in the lungs. If we catch anything early, we can adjust her treatment. Given it's still very early, adjusting her treatment now will assure us of a good prognosis."

Dr. Patel, the neurosurgeon, feeling the need to brighten the mood in the room, did a quick assessment of Linda's coma score.

"We're also monitoring her neurological status closely. As we reduce the sedation, we'll be checking for any early signs of responsiveness. So far, she's picking up. That could explain the stress on her body."

Nancy leaned forward, absorbing the information. "So, we can still be hopeful."

Dr. Faulkner's expression was calm, moving around the bed to the ventilator. "It's not uncommon for patients on ventilators to experience setbacks," he said as he adjusted the machine, turning the dials.

"The good news is that we're catching it early. Once we get the ABG results, we'll know more and we can give her medications if needed."

Nancy exhaled slowly, her shoulders relaxing slightly. It wasn't the worst news, but it was still unsettling. Linda was alive and fighting, but the road to recovery was full of unknowns.

Dr. Roberts, the orthopedic surgeon, who had been silently observing all the events, looked at Nancy.

"The good thing is that her other vitals are stable. That gives us more confidence that she can tolerate the surgery on her leg once her head injury is stable and thus respiratory issues are addressed," he added.

Nancy nodded, grateful for the doctor's transparency. "Thank you for explaining all this. I was beginning to get really worried."

Dr. Patel offered a reassuring smile. "We'll take it one step at a time. Like we said previously, Linda is in good hands."

Dr. Faulkner scribbled some notes on the chart and gave one last look at the monitor. "We'll have the results in about an hour. I'll come back to update you as soon as we know more."

Nancy lingered at the doorway, her fingers gripping the frame as if it could anchor her against the wave of emotion threatening to pull her under. She took a slow, steady breath, willing herself to stay composed before stepping inside.

The air was heavy with the sterile scent of antiseptic, the steady beep of monitors the only sound breaking the stillness. The woman lying in the bed looked nothing like the Linda she knew. Her face, usually so full of life, was ghostly pale, marred by deep bruises. Wires and tubes snaked around her, machines taking over the body that once moved with such energy. The sight hit Nancy like a physical blow.

Barbara sat at her daughter's bedside, her fingers clenched together so tightly that her knuckles had turned white. Her gaze never wavered from Linda's face, as if sheer determination could will her back to consciousness. The weight of the past twenty-four hours had etched new lines into her face, her exhaustion palpable.

In the corner, Tom was slumped in a chair, head tilted back, mouth slightly open. Asleep—or passed out. Nancy clenched her jaw, swallowing the irritation that rose in her throat. Now wasn't the time for resentment.

She moved closer, dragging a chair to Linda's bedside, her heart clenching at how fragile she looked.

Barbara stirred at the sound, blinking as if waking from a trance. She turned to Nancy, offering a weary smile. "You're back," she whispered, her voice hoarse from too many tears and too little rest.

Nancy nodded. "I'm here."

For a long moment, neither of them spoke. Then Nancy reached out, taking Barbara's cold hand in hers. "You should go home for a little while. Shower, eat something, check on the kids. They need you too."

Barbara's lips pressed into a thin line, her grip tightening around Nancy's hand. "I don't know if I can leave her."

"I know," Nancy said gently. "But you have to take care of yourself too. I'll stay with her. She won't be alone."

Barbara exhaled shakily, her body sagging under the weight of exhaustion. For a moment, it seemed like she might protest, but then she simply nodded.

Nancy watched as she gathered her things, moving slowly, hesitantly. When she finally stepped out of the room, Nancy turned back to Linda. She reached for her hand, cool and unmoving beneath her touch.

"Come back to us, Linda. We're all waiting."

Chapter Seven:
Families

Barbara and Tom left the medical center and walked through the parking lot to Tom's truck. Once inside the truck Barbara began asking questions.

"Where were you really last night?"

"I told you I was out with the boys."

"Where exactly and what were you doing so that you missed supper and came home very late?"

We were at Ray's Roadhouse having a few beers and playing cards. I lost track of time, but you have no reason to ask what I do or where I go as long as I provide a good living. So, stop questioning me,"!

"Well, you could at least call me if you're going to be late,"!

I am an adult man and I can go wherever I want whenever I want without notifying you,"!

"If it makes you feel any better, Father Thomas was there too. He wasn't gambling but he was sure putting the Scotch away."

"Alright enough of that. Let's stop at Linda's house and see how the kids are doing. Brenda is only 16. It's a lot of responsibility for her to take care of all those kids. Maybe we should bring them over to our house."

"Okay."

They drove in silence the rest of the way. When they got to Linda's Tom pulled into the driveway and they both got out. They walked into the house to behold a mess beyond belief. Toys everywhere, spilled food on the floor and table, dirty dishes in the sink and the kids running wild.

"Oh my God Brenda what has been going on all day?" Barbara asked.

"I was up all night worrying about Mom and I finally fell asleep. When I woke up a little while ago this was the mess they had created.

"Okay, you little kids pick up all your toys and put them away. Daniel, you help them. Linda, you clean up the table and floor while I do the dishes," Barbara ordered.

"When you are done, you're all coming home with us. It's obvious you need more supervision."

"Grandma", Brenda said, "you can take the three little ones but Daniel and I are staying here."

"Why"?

"I don't like how Grandpa drinks all the time and you two fight. Daniel and I can take care of ourselves."

"Alright, you pack up some clothes for them, but we will be checking on you and Daniel every day. And you need to go back to school."

"We will next week when Mom is better."

"We'll talk about school later."

When the clean-up was satisfactory and the kids' clothes were packed, Barbara and Tom loaded the kids and the clothes into the truck and headed home.

"You are not going out drinking tonight, Tom. I need help taking care of these children,"!

"Okay, okay. I'll watch a movie with them and you get them ready for bed. Deal?"

" Fine."

Back at the medical center, Nancy sat beside Linda's bed, her fingers gently wrapped around her friend's still hand. The steady rhythm of the monitors filled the room, an almost hypnotic reminder that Linda was still here, still fighting.

She sighed, leaning forward slightly. *"I don't know if you can hear me, Linda, but I'm here. We all are. You just need to wake up, okay? We need you back."*

The soft creak of the door interrupted the quiet moment. She turned to see Father Thomas stepping inside, his presence bringing a rare sense of calm to the heavy atmosphere.

"How's she doing?" he asked, his voice low and gentle.

Nancy exhaled. "She's had some serious injuries, but right now, she's stable."

Father Thomas nodded, stepping closer. "She doesn't come to church often, but I baptized her, did her first communion, and confirmed her. It's part of my job to visit parishioners in the medical center." His expression was thoughtful, eyes resting on Linda with quiet concern.

Nancy glanced at him, surprised. "I didn't know that."

He offered a small smile. "Even if she wasn't a regular, she's still part of the flock." He paused before adding, "Her nurse told me you were here all night with her mother and came back this evening to relieve her. You must be exhausted."

Nancy let out a tired chuckle. "Exhausted doesn't even cover it." She ran a hand through her hair. "But Barbara needed a break. She wouldn't leave unless someone was here."

Father Thomas studied her for a moment, then pulled up a chair beside her. "That kind of loyalty is rare."

Nancy looked back at Linda, squeezing her hand gently. "She's worth it."

"I would be glad to stay with Linda so you can go home and get some rest, you must have to work tomorrow."

"Are you sure you don't mind?"

"Mind?" It's my job and I need to be here if her condition changes. You take a much-needed break and I will take over."

"Thank you so much. I need the rest and I haven't been spending enough time with my children the past two days."

Nancy left the medical center and drove home feeling slightly guilty about leaving Linda, but knowing she needed to spend some time with her children and to get some more sleep.

When Nancy got home, the familiar hum of the television filled the house. She stepped into the family room and immediately spotted the mess—popcorn scattered across the rug like fallen confetti. Her children, lounging on the couch, turned to her with wide eyes, clearly not expecting her back so soon.

She sighed, pressing her fingers to her temples. *Not tonight. I don't have the energy for this.*

"Well," she said, crossing her arms, "I'm glad to see you all got your homework done and are ready for bed." Her voice carried more exhaustion than irritation. "Because frankly, I'm too tired to discuss your assignments—or this disaster on my rug."

The kids exchanged guilty glances, shifting awkwardly.

"I'm going to wash up and go to bed," she continued. "When I get up for work in the morning, I don't want to see *so much as a single popcorn seed* on that rug." She gave them a pointed look. "Clean up, get ready, and go to bed. No arguments."

Without waiting for a response, she turned and headed for the stairs, too drained to deal with anything else. Behind her, she heard the TV click off and the soft rustle of her kids scrambling to clean up. *Small victories,* she thought as she disappeared into her room.

Chapter Eight:
Morning Rounds

Barbara and Tom entered the medical center early, navigating the quiet halls of the ICU with heavy steps. The scent of antiseptic hung in the cold and sterile air. Barbara's gaze lingered on Linda through the glass window of her room, her heart aching at the sight of her daughter lying so still under the machines that kept her alive.

Father Thomas sat at the bedside praying. He looked up and tried to force a smile as Barbara and Tom approached.

"You're here," he said softly, rising from his seat. He stretched, his joints cracking from hours of sitting in the stiff chair. "I should head home, shower, and get some rest. I'll come back later tonight."

Barbara gave him a grateful smile. "Thank you, Father. You've really been very helpful. We're here this early so that you can get some sleep at home before doing your work."

He gave Barbara a warm hug, then walked out of the room, his tired steps following him down the corridor.

As the door clicked shut behind him, Barbara sat down in the chair the priest had vacated. She took Linda's hand gently in hers, brushing her thumb over her daughter's skin.

Tom remained standing by the window, his hands jammed into his jacket pockets. His eyes were fixed on the machines surrounding Linda: the ventilator, the monitors, the tangle of wires. He shifted his weight uncomfortably, as if the beeping of the monitors were drilling into his skull.

Barbara glanced at him. "She's so fragile, Tom. I keep thinking, "What if she doesn't make it?"

Tom sighed, still staring out the window. "Don't talk like that, Barb. She's tough. She'll pull through."

Barbara's eyes filled with tears, and her voice was shaky. "It's just that I've seen cases like this in movies. Even if she survives, what if she's not the same?"

"But this is not a movie," Tom replied impatiently.

He turned from the window, his expression tight. "We'll take it one day at a time. Worrying about what might happen won't change anything."

Barbara swallowed hard, biting back her fears. "But we should…"

Before she could finish, the door opened, and the doctors walked in, interrupting their conversation. Dr. Faulkner, the pulmonologist, led the way, his clipboard tucked under his arm. Dr. Patel, the neurosurgeon, followed close behind.

Barbara stood up quickly, wiping at her eyes. "Good morning, doctors."

"Good morning," Dr. Faulkner said, nodding politely. "I wanted to update you on Linda's condition." He noticed she's looking around for their third colleague. "Our orthopedic surgeon, Dr Roberts, won't be joining us today. He was called into an emergency surgery this morning."

Barbara nodded, though she felt a twinge of unease. "I hope the result doesn't indicate something too serious."

Dr. Patel offered a reassuring smile, the kind that softened but didn't erase worry. "No, nothing like that. We just wanted to check in and go over her progress with you."

Barbara exhaled, relief trickling in, but she didn't let her guard down completely. She had learned not to. "Alright," she said, nodding. "Please—tell me how she's doing."

Now, let's go over Linda's test results from last evening." He flipped through the pages on his clipboard, his tone becoming more clinical. "We performed an arterial blood gas test and a chest X-ray, which confirmed what we suspected. Linda has developed pneumonia."

Tom let out a low-toned whistle. "Pneumonia?" he asked.

"Yes," Dr. Faulkner said. "It's not uncommon for patients who are on mechanical ventilation. The lack of natural breathing can lead to fluid buildup in the lungs, which, unfortunately, creates a breeding ground for bacteria."

Barbara's face tightened

"What does that mean? How serious is it?"

"It's a setback, but it's manageable," Dr. Faulkner reassured her. "We've already started her on broad-spectrum antibiotics to fight the infection. We'll monitor her closely, adjusting the medication based on how she responds. She'll also remain on the ventilator for now to support her breathing while we manage the pneumonia."

Barbara exhaled, though her anxiety remained. "How long will it take for the infection to clear?"

"It's hard to say," Dr. Faulkner admitted. "We're catching it early, which is a good thing, but every patient responds differently. We'll know more in a day or two based on her progress."

Dr. Patel, the neurosurgeon, stepped forward, his expression serious but calm. "There's one other thing I need to discuss," he said gently. "We've decided to keep Linda in a medically induced coma for now."

Tom's head jerked up. "Why? I thought the goal was to reduce sedation and see if she's responsive."

Before Barbara could finish her thought, the door creaked open, and the doctors strode in, their presence immediately shifting the energy in the room. Dr. Faulkner, the pulmonologist, led the way, his clipboard tucked under his arm, his expression neutral but purposeful. Dr. Patel, the neurosurgeon, followed closely behind, his sharp eyes scanning the room before settling on Linda.

Barbara shot to her feet, wiping at her eyes quickly, trying to compose herself. "Good morning, doctors." Her voice wavered slightly, but she steadied it.

"Good morning," Dr. Faulkner replied with a polite nod. His voice was even, measured—the kind of tone that was meant to reassure, though Barbara had learned that didn't always mean good news. "I wanted to update you on Linda's condition."

She glanced at the doorway, instinctively searching for Dr. Roberts. Noticing her concern, Dr. Faulkner spoke before she could ask. "Our orthopedic surgeon, Dr. Roberts, won't be joining us today. He was called into emergency surgery this morning."

Barbara nodded, but a flicker of unease tightened in her chest. She swallowed, forcing herself to sound calm. "I hope that doesn't mean…" She hesitated, pressing a hand against her stomach. "I hope the results don't indicate something more serious."

Dr. Patel offered a reassuring smile, the kind that softened but didn't erase worry. "No, nothing like that. We just wanted to check in and go over her progress with you."

Barbara exhaled, relief trickling in, but she didn't let her guard down completely. She had learned not to. "Alright," she said, nodding. "Please—tell me how she's doing."

Dr. Faulkner gave a sympathetic smile. "I know it's hard, but we're doing everything we can. Linda is strong. With time and the right care, she has a good chance of recovery."

"Thank you, doctors," Barbara said.

Dr. Patel gave her a kind nod. "We'll keep you updated on her progress. If you have any questions or concerns, don't hesitate to ask."

With that, the two doctors gave a final glance at Linda's monitors before making their way to the door. "We'll check on her again this afternoon," Dr. Faulkner added as they left.

As the door closed behind the doctors, the room fell into silence again. Barbara sat down heavily in the chair by Linda's bedside, pressing her hand to her chest as if to hold her emotions together.

Chapter Nine:
Tom Goes to Work

After Tom listened to what the doctors had to say he told his wife he was going to work. "I can't leave Brian alone to pump gas and do all the repairs anymore. And I need to fix your car so you have transportation," he said.

"Okay, but you have to be home when the kids get out of school and make sure they come to our house,"

Tom gave a small nod, as if relieved to have her permission. "I'll see you later," he said, turning toward the door and headed out of the room.

He stopped, turned and said, "Don't worry, I will make sure the kids are safe and fed. Please call me if there is any change in Linda's condition."

"I will if I can find you."

Tom turned back and left.

When he arrived at the garage Brian looked worn out.

"I'm so sorry about your daughter. It's been pretty hard keeping up with everything, but I'll do whatever you need."

"First I need to fix my wife's car so she has transportation to the medical center."

"I saw those parts under the drop cloth. What happened?"

"I hit something. I think it was a deer."

"You're in luck because I ordered the parts and they should be here this afternoon."

"What else are you working on?"

"I've got a brake job lined up, and there's a new guy in town who needs his transmission checked. If it doesn't need repairs, I'll just change the fluid. I've also got a few inspections scheduled for tomorrow, plus a tune-up for someone," he said, wiping his hands on a rag. "Didn't want to overload myself until I knew when you'd be back."

"I'll have to leave when my grandkids get out of school," the older man replied, adjusting his cap. "But if the parts come in, I'll get started on that job so Barbara will have transportation. You can finish it up after I head out."

He sighed, running a hand over his graying beard. "That way, I can visit my daughter in the morning and after work, while Barbara takes care of the kids." His voice softened, the weight of responsibility pressing on his shoulders.

The parts for Barbara's car arrived at noon. Tom replaced the light and made sure it worked. He removed the old fender and put that on and it was nearing 3 pm.

"Hey Brian," he said. "I fixed the light and the fender. Can you replace the front bumper and take it for a test drive?"

"Sure, I'll do that, bring it to your house and you can give me a ride back to the garage."

"Thanks."

Tom left and the kids were at his house.

"You guys want a snack and then you can play outside for a while."

"Thanks, Grandpa," they chorused.

Tom called the medical center and asked for ICU. He identified himself and asked to speak to his wife. They transferred the call to Linda's room. He told her he would fix dinner, but was Nancy working and could she give Barbara a ride home?

"She is working and I'm sure she will give me a ride home. Just feed the kids and check to see if they have any homework. After their homework is done, have them get ready for bed and watch a movie with them. I'll put them to bed when I get home."

.   .

.

Meanwhile, back at Linda's house, Brenda and Daniel stayed home and watched TV. Luckily, Brenda knew how to cook so they had lunch and dinner together.

Brenda had been acting worried and fidgety all day. She answered Daniel's questions with monosyllables and couldn't seem to follow the TV programs.

Finally, Daniel said," What's wrong with you today? You've been acting restless and nervous all day. You won't talk to me and I know you're not really watching the TV."

"No," said Daniel. "It's more than that."

Brenda burst into tears which made Daniel feel terrible. Just then, the phone rang. Daniel answered. It was their grandmother.

"Did you go to school today?"

"No, Brenda is really upset and she couldn't face answering a lot of questions from her classmates. She's been acting funny all day and when I asked her what was wrong, she started crying."

"She's worried about your mother."

"I know she is, but it's more than that."

"Have you got food and have you eaten?"

"Yes, Grandma, we made our own lunches and Brenda cooked dinner. We're all set."

"Nothing has really changed with your mother. She's still in a coma. I will be home late tonight, but I will check on you tomorrow."

Daniel went back to Brenda who had somewhat composed herself.

"Please tell me what's wrong? he asked.

"I want to," she said, "but I'm afraid," she replied.

"Are you pregnant?" he asked.

"NO"!

"Then what are you afraid of?"

"I saw something, but I am not 100% sure and I'm afraid if I tell you, you will tell Grandma."

"I promise, no matter what it is, I won't tell anyone."

"You won't tell no matter what it is?"

" I promise,"!

"I will never forgive you if you do."

"What is it?"

"When Steve and I were driving home from our date, I saw a car that looked just like Mom's. A man was driving it... and he kind of looked like Grandpa," she said, her voice hesitant, like she was piecing the memory together in real time.

She swallowed hard before continuing. "He swerved to miss us—right around the spot where Mom was found. And now, I can't stop thinking... what if Grandpa hit her?" Her chest tightened at the thought, the words feeling heavier now that they were out in the open.

"He told us he hit a deer and that's what damaged Grandma's car, but..." She shook her head. "I didn't see any deer anywhere near that road."

. .
.

After the phone call with Daniel, Barbara went to check with Nancy about a ride home. When she found her, she asked when her shift ended and if it would be convenient to give her a ride home.

"I get off at about 7:30 and I would be happy to give you a ride home," Nancy answered.

After the report was given, it was about 8 pm. Nancy went into Linda's room. Barbara was sitting next to the bed holding Linda's hand.

"I am ready to go home now, Barbara, if you still want a ride," Nancy offered.

"Barbara got up, kissed Linda's forehead, and said, "I'll be back soon, sweetie. You rest and get well."

Barbara then grabbed her purse and followed Nancy out of the medical center.

"I talked to Linda's nurse, Susan, and she said Linda is stabilizing and seems to be improving," Nancy said as they walked to her car. "What did the doctors say?"

"The doctors said she is holding her own. Her breathing is better and they want to repair her broken thigh.

As they headed to Nancy's car, Father Tomas drove up.

"Hi Father Thomas, I see you're back again."

"I try to come daily to relieve Barbara and pray for Linda," he said.

"That's so nice of you."

Noticing the priest's car was green not blue, did you buy a new car?" Nancy asked.

"No, that's a loaner. They are doing some work on my car at the dealership."

"Thank you so much for relieving me, Father Thomas. I feel so much better knowing she's not alone," Barbara said.

"I'll do anything to help my parishioners," said Father Thomas as he headed to the medical center.

Barbara and Nancy got into Nancy's car, the hum of the engine filling the comfortable silence between them as they headed home. The day had been long, draining in every possible way, but for the first time in a while, Barbara felt a small sense of relief.

"Tom said my car should be ready tomorrow," Barbara said, glancing over at Nancy. "You've been such a help—I'm going to ask him to give you a discount on your repairs."

Nancy shook her head with a small smile. "That's very kind, but it's not necessary. I would have done this for any of my neighbors." She hesitated, choosing her words carefully. She didn't mention her new job starting next week—the one Linda had wanted so badly. It didn't feel right to bring it up now.

"Still," Barbara insisted, her voice softer now, "we want to show our appreciation. You've done so much for us."

Nancy didn't argue, only nodding as she pulled into Barbara's driveway.

Barbara opened the door and stepped out, then turned back, resting a hand on the frame. "Thank you, Nancy. For everything."

Nancy gave her a reassuring smile. "Get some rest, Barbara. I'll check in tomorrow."

Barbara nodded, shutting the door gently behind her as Nancy drove off into the night.

Chapter Ten:
JJ Continues Investigating

Detective Jason pulled into the medical center parking lot, muttering curses under his breath. He scanned the rows of parked cars, his irritation growing as he circled around for what felt like the tenth time. Finally, he spotted a tight space between a minivan and a beat-up sedan. With a sharp turn of the wheel, he slid the car in expertly.

"Should've joined the circus," he muttered, stepping out and slamming the door behind him.

The October sun hung high, its golden rays bouncing off the glass facade of the medical center. JJ adjusted the collar of his leather jacket, the worn material creaking slightly as he strode toward the entrance. His steps were unhurried, measured—the kind of effortless confidence that turned heads without trying.

Inside, the cool air carried the sterile scent of antiseptic, a sharp contrast to the crisp autumn breeze outside. He pulled off his sunglasses, tucking them into his jacket pocket as his sharp gaze swept across the reception area. The soft hum of conversation and the occasional beeping of monitors filled the space, but he wasn't here to linger.

Behind the desk, a young blonde receptionist glanced up, her lips curling into a polite, almost intrigued smile. JJ returned a subtle nod, his expression unreadable, though he made a mental note—charm was a currency, and he'd be cashing in on his way out.

For now, though, business came first.

"I'm here to speak to the doctors in charge of Linda Berry's case," he said, approaching the desk.

The receptionist typed briskly into her computer. "Are you family?"

"Detective Jason," JJ said, flipping open his badge with a practiced flick. "Investigating officer on the hit-and-run case."

"Oh, of course," she replied, her smile lingering a little longer than necessary. "You'll find most of them in their offices this time of day. I'll print out the room numbers for you."

JJ took the slip she handed him, giving her a wink. "Thanks, sweetheart."

Her cheeks flushed pink, and JJ turned away, chuckling under his breath.

. .
.

JJ navigated the maze of medical center corridors, finding the first office on his list - Dr. Patel, the neurosurgeon. He knocked on the door and waited for a response.

Dr. Patel sat behind a desk with medical charts scattered around, his dark eyes sharp behind his large glasses. "Detective, come in," he said, setting a file aside.

JJ stepped inside, closing the door behind him. "Thanks for taking the time, Doc. I just have a few questions about your patient, Linda Berry."

Dr. Patel gestured to a chair, and JJ sat down, notebook ready.

"Can you give me your take on the injuries?" JJ asked. "And I'm interested in whether you can estimate the time of the accident or explain how these injuries might have occurred."

Dr. Patel folded his hands. "From my perspective, her most serious injury is the intracerebral hemorrhage. The injury suggests significant trauma to the head. Such can either occur from direct impact or from a secondary collision, like being thrown against a hard surface."

JJ jotted down notes. "Any idea what kind of force we're talking about?"

"Considerable. The force could have been from either a fast-moving vehicle or from her hitting the ground with her head after impact. Given the nature of her injuries, I would estimate the accident occurred 30 minutes to 1 hour before she was found. But that's just my guess - it can vary considerably."

JJ nodded. "So, we're looking at a high-speed collision?"

"Possibly. The head injuries alone would've rendered her unconscious almost immediately."

JJ leaned forward. "And what's the prognosis?"

Dr. Patel sighed. "We'll keep her in an induced coma for now to reduce brain swelling. If she wakes up, there could be cognitive deficits or motor impairments. But it's too early to tell."

JJ tapped his pen against the notepad, processing the information. "Thanks, Doc. That helps. I'll be in touch in case I need further information."

He stood up, shook hands with Dr Patel, and walked back into the corridor.

. .
.

JJ eased into the chair across from Dr. Faulkner's desk, ignoring the brief flicker of disapproval in the doctor's gaze at his uninvited seating. The office was neat and sterile, the faint scent of coffee lingering in the air.

"I need your insight on Linda Berry's condition," JJ said, his voice steady but pressing. "What's the state of her lungs, and can you tell me anything about the timing of the accident?"

Dr. Faulkner set his pen down and leaned back slightly, his fingers threading together over his stomach. His lab coat was crisp, his posture composed—a man accustomed to delivering clinical truths without embellishment.

"Her primary respiratory concern right now is pneumonia," he said. "It's likely a complication from being on the ventilator. But it's also possible the accident played a role. Trauma victims who lose consciousness sometimes aspirate, which can introduce bacteria into the lungs."

JJ's jaw tightened slightly. "So you can't say for sure if the pneumonia is from the accident or the ventilator?"

Faulkner shook his head. "Not definitively. But given the timeline, it's a mix of both."

JJ exhaled, nodding slowly. This wasn't the answer he wanted, but it was something. A piece of the puzzle—one he'd have to fit into the bigger picture himself.

"Can you narrow down when she might have been hit?" JJ asked.

"The respiratory data alone wouldn't help with that," Dr. Faulkner said. "But I can say that if she aspirated during the accident, that would suggest she lost consciousness at the moment of impact."

JJ scribbled notes; his brow furrowed. "And how's she doing now?"

"We've started antibiotics for the pneumonia," Dr. Faulkner replied. "If her body responds, she should improve over the next few days. But it's a delicate situation. Any complications could slow her recovery.

JJ stood and extended a hand. "Thanks for your time, Doc. I'll see you again if I need further details."

Dr. Faulkner gave a curt nod, returning to his paperwork.

. .
.

The last stop was the orthopedic surgeon's office.

Dr Roberts was sitting in his chair, sipping from a water bottle. His surgical scrubs were wrinkled, and there were faint circles under his eyes.

"Hello, detective, how are you?" Dr. Roberts said as JJ stepped inside.

"Can't complain." JJ said as he walked into the office and sank into a chair.

"I just finished a surgery. I hope this won't take long."

"I'll be quick," JJ assured him, pulling out his notebook. "I need your take on Linda Berry's injuries. I've talked with the neurosurgeon and pulmonologist, and now I need your insight."

Dr. Roberts leaned forward, rubbing his hands together. "Linda has a fractured femur and several broken ribs. From what I can tell, the fractures are consistent with high-impact trauma - likely a car accident.

JJ nodded, jotting down notes. "How severe are the fractures?"

"The femur was completely broken, and two ribs were fractured on the left side. We've stabilized the leg with an external fixator, but she'll need definitive surgery when she's stable enough."

JJ glanced up. "What about the ribs? Could they have punctured her lung?"

Dr. Roberts shook his head. "No puncture, but the fractures are likely contributing to her breathing issues. It's not surprising she developed pneumonia. Injuries like this often restrict a patient's ability to breathe deeply, which makes them prone to lung infections."

"Can you tell me anything about the timing of the accident?" JJ asked, leaning forward.

Dr. Roberts paused, considering. "Based on the bruising around the fractures, I'd say the accident happened about 1 to 2 hours before she was admitted. That's consistent with trauma injuries we see from accidents."

"Could these injuries have been caused by anything other than a car accident?" JJ asked.

"Unlikely," Dr. Roberts replied. "The force needed to break a femur like that would require either a high-speed collision or a heavy object hitting her. The rib fractures, combined with the leg injury, suggest she was struck on one side, then either thrown or pinned."

JJ scribbled the final notes. "Got it. So, she's going to need surgery again?"

"Eventually, yes," Dr. Roberts said. "But right now, our priority is stabilizing her overall condition. She'll need intensive physical therapy once she wakes up."

JJ stood, offering a handshake. "Thanks, Doc. You've been a big help."

Dr. Roberts gave a tired smile. "If you need anything else, let me know. But I hope next time you come; it's not about another patient."

Satisfied with the interviews, JJ made his way back toward the reception desk. He replayed the doctors' words in his mind, piecing together the puzzle: The head injury pointed to a fast-moving collision. The pneumonia was a complication, but not likely related to the time of the accident.

It wasn't a perfect picture, but it was clearer than before. Now he had a rough timeline - Linda was likely hit 1 to 2 hours before she was found, unconscious, by Nancy. That gave him a window to work with, narrowing down the list of potential suspects and their alibis.

As JJ reached the front desk, the receptionist looked up from her computer, her eyes lighting up when she saw him. JJ gave her a grin, pausing just long enough to make her day.

"Thanks for your help earlier," he said, giving her a playful wink.

The young woman blushed. "Anytime, Detective."

With a final nod, JJ pushed through the glass doors, stepping back into the parking lot. He slipped on his sunglasses and made his way back to his car. He slid into the driver's seat, started the engine, and pulled out of the lot.

Chapter Eleven:
Nancy's New Job

N ancy made sure the kids were ready for school, checking that they had their homework, lunches or lunch money and were ready for the bus. "I'm sorry to be rushing you, she said, but I start my new job today and I don't want to be late."

"Don't forget to let Cody out when you get home and then feed him." She left for work.

As Nancy crossed the parking lot, the crisp morning air did little to shake the exhaustion clinging to her bones. She spotted Father Thomas unlocking his car, his shoulders heavy with fatigue. He had been a near-constant presence at the hospital, keeping vigil beside Linda when Barbara couldn't.

He glanced up as she approached, offering a tired but warm smile. She returned it with a small wave.

Nancy shook off the thought and quickened her pace, pushing through the ICU doors. The scent of antiseptic and coffee—burnt and bitter—filled the air. She made her way to her office, dropping her purse onto the chair before grabbing a blank sheet of paper. There was no time to settle in. Report was about to start.

As she walked through the nurses' station to listen to report, the ICU secretary told her Mrs. Collins, the Director of Nursing, wanted to see her.

Nancy practically ran down the corridor to Mrs. Collins' office. When she entered the waiting area, Mrs. Collins' secretary told her to have a seat. Mrs. Collins would be right with her.

Shortly, Mrs. Collins opened her door and motioned for Nancy to enter.

Nancy swallowed hard as she stepped into the office, her pulse quickening. Mrs. Collins, the Director of Nurses, was a woman of quiet authority, her every movement deliberate. The office was neat, save for the stack of papers she was sorting through. A faint scent of coffee lingered in the air.

"Have a seat," Mrs. Collins said, gesturing to the chair across from her.

Nancy eased into the chair, smoothing her skirt with damp palms. She willed herself to stay composed, but a nervous energy hummed beneath her skin. This was it—the first official conversation in her new role.

Mrs. Collins finished straightening her papers and folded her hands over them, her sharp eyes settling on Nancy.

"I'll get straight to the point," she said. "You have an excellent reputation here, and I have high expectations. The ICU can be unpredictable, and you'll need to be ready for anything. How are you feeling about stepping into this role?"

Nancy straightened her shoulders, meeting Mrs. Collins' gaze. "I'm ready," she said, her voice steadier than she expected. "I know it'll be demanding, but I'm prepared to handle it."

Mrs. Collins nodded, her expression unreadable. "Good. Let's talk about what that means in practice."

Nancy braced herself, knowing that whatever came next would set the tone for everything ahead.

When they were both settled, Mrs. Collin handed Nancy a thick sheaf of papers and said, "This is your job description, which I know you have read before. However, I would like you to go over it again today, reading in detail your responsibilities. If you have any questions, please call me so I can make sure you understand everything."

"Your ICU protocols are in a booklet in your office and you should review them also. In addition, the locked bottom drawer of your file cabinet has confidential files of complaints, errors made and files on every ICU nurse to name a few. You can browse through them later at your leisure. Here is the key to that drawer and the key to your office, both of which you are responsible for keeping safe.".

Next, Mrs. Collins handed her several more papers." These are the dates, times and locations of all the meetings you must attend unless there is an emergency in ICU," she told her.

"Do you have any questions?" Mrs. Collins asked.

"I can't think of any right now, but I am sure I will have a lot of questions in the future."

Mrs. Collins stood up and held out her hand. Nancy shook her hand as Mrs. Collins said, "I am pleased you applied for and accepted this position, Nancy. You have been an excellent ICU nurse and a valuable and intelligent employee. I am sure you will do a great job and I look forward to working with you."

"Thank you," Nancy replied. "I will do my best to live up to your expectations."

Nancy headed back to ICU and unlocked her office door. She put the two keys on the key chain where she kept her house and car keys, thinking she must find a safe place at home to store them. As she sat down at her desk, she saw an envelope with her name on it.

She opened the envelope and there was a short letter from the former Director of ICU, Molly. It read:

Dear Nancy,

Sorry, I didn't get to speak to you in person, but my baby came a little sooner than expected.

Welcome to your new position. It can be difficult at times, but I am sure you will do a great job.

I am happy to be home with my baby. Though I will miss many of my friends, I hope they will come to visit and/or we can get together for dinner or drinks.

I will not be getting much sleep for a while, but if you have any questions, don't hesitate to call me. I am more than willing to support you.

Best of luck,

Molly.

Nancy smiled as she read the neatly penned note left on her desk. The former ICU director, Lisa, had given birth earlier than expected, leaving behind this message in lieu of a proper farewell.

She traced the edge of the paper with her fingertips, feeling a mix of excitement and the weight of responsibility settle over her.

She could almost hear Lisa's voice in the words—warm, and encouraging, but also laced with the honesty of someone who knew exactly what this job demanded.

Nancy exhaled, folding the letter and putting it in her purse. She appreciated the offer of support, but she was determined to stand on her own.

Still, she made a mental note to send Lisa a message later—congratulating her and thanking her for the thoughtful welcome.

For now, though, it was time to get to work.

She left the job description on her desk and pinned the meetings schedule to her bulletin board. She would enter them into her phone reminders later.

Nancy got out of her chair and headed to the nurses' station of ICU. "Who's in charge today?" she asked the secretary.

"Susan," she replied.

Nancy went to look for Susan who also happened to be her best friend. She found her in a patient's room talking to a patient.

"Excuse me for interrupting," Nancy said. "Susan. could you come to my office when You are finished here?"

"I'll be there shortly," Susan replied.

Nancy went back to her office and started reading her responsibilities in her job description. After about 5 minutes Susan knocked on the open door.

"Are you busy or do you have time to give me a report on the patients," Nancy asked?

"I have time let me get my worksheet."

Susan returned with her worksheet. "Before we begin, she said, you have to tell me how things are going with JJ."

"We've been out a few times and I enjoy his company but we're both so busy we mostly talk on the phone."

"When are you going to see him again?"

I was thinking of inviting him to my house for dinner. I need to spend more time with my kids and I am anxious to see how they react to him."

"That's a great Idea. I hope he accepts your invitation and the kids like him."

"Okay, enough. Report please."

Susan began reading off the room numbers, names, ages, sex and diagnoses of each patient.

When she got to Linda, Nancy had a lot of questions.

Susan said, "I'm sorry I missed the doctors when they made rounds on her. We were still in report. But honestly, I don't see much change. She's still in a coma and on the ventilator.

Nancy frowned, tapping her pen lightly against her notepad. "Still no response at all?"

Susan shook her head. "Not that I've seen. Vitals are stable, but no real signs of improvement."

Nancy let out a slow breath. She hated the waiting game—watching families cling to hope, balancing realism with the possibility of a miracle. "I'll check in with Dr. Faulkner and Dr. Patel later. Maybe they'll have something new."

Susan hesitated before adding, "Her mom's been in and out all day. She barely left her side."

"I'm not surprised," Nancy murmured. Barbara had been holding on with everything she had.

For a moment, there was silence between them. Then Susan smirked. "So, back to something a little more fun— when's this dinner happening?"

Nancy rolled her eyes but couldn't fight the small smile tugging at her lips. "I haven't asked him yet. We'll see."

"Better hurry before he thinks you're playing hard to get," Susan teased before handing Nancy her notes and heading back to work.

Shaking her head, Nancy turned back to the patient list, but her thoughts lingered on Linda—and, for just a moment, on JJ.

Chapter Twelve:
Pneumonia Improved:
Thigh Surgery

Blood Results:

Nancy Talks to the Priest

JJ Talks to the Family

Barbara sat at her daughter Linda's bedside, clutching her hand gently. Next to her, Tom leaned against the wall, arms crossed. He looked weary, as if sleep had eluded him. Nancy stood a little to the side, looking at her watch occasionally. Her new job required her to leave soon, and she wouldn't be staying overnight anymore - a change she knew Barbara and Tom understood but one she still felt guilty about.

Linda's face remained peaceful, her body still under the influence of induced sedation.

Barbara sighed. Every minute in the medical center felt like a lifetime.

Nancy cleared her throat gently. "I'll only be coming in the mornings from now on," she said, glancing at Barbara and Tom. "I can't stay late. This new job is demanding."

Barbara gave her a warm smile. "We're just grateful you can come at all."

Tom nodded but said nothing. His mind seemed elsewhere, likely in the familiar clutter of his garage, where problems were mechanical, not emotional. He knew the coming hours were crucial for Linda.

A soft knock interrupted their quiet moment. The door swung open, and the ward round team entered: the three doctors walked in, with an internist trailing behind, reviewing Linda's latest lab results and vital signs.

Barbara and Tom straightened as the doctors walked in, and Nancy folded her arms, prepared to absorb every word.

Dr. Faulkner nodded, glancing at Linda's monitors. "Her lung function is improving. The pneumonia is responding to treatment, and we've been able to reduce the ventilator settings slightly."

Barbara let out a breath she hadn't realized she was holding. "That's wonderful."

Dr. Patel, the neurosurgeon, stepped forward. "We still have a long road ahead. Neurologically, there's been no significant change. She remains unresponsive, but we're continuing to monitor her brain activity closely."

Tom cleared his throat. "So, what does that mean? Are we talking days, weeks?"

Dr. Patel exchanged a glance with Dr. Faulkner before replying carefully. "It's impossible to predict with certainty. But stabilization is a good sign."

Nancy's grip on her arms tightened. She'd seen cases like this before—where every small step forward still left the future uncertain. "And the next steps?" she asked.

Dr. Faulkner adjusted his glasses. "If her respiratory status continues to improve, we'll start discussing weaning her off the ventilator in the coming days. But for now, we continue as we are."

Barbara wiped at her eyes, nodding. "Thank you. Just knowing she's improving, even a little, means everything."

The doctors offered small, reassuring smiles before moving on to their next patient. As the door closed behind them, Barbara exhaled shakily, turning to Nancy.

"You think she hears us?" she whispered.

Nancy reached for Linda's hand, squeezing it gently. "I do. And I think she knows we're all here, waiting for her."

Nancy let out a small sigh of relief. "Thank you, Doctor," she said sincerely. "That's such a relief to hear."

Tom shifted from his spot by the wall, finally engaging. "So, what's next?"

The neurosurgeon, Dr. Patel, quickly added: "Linda's neurological status remains stable. She still needs to stay under sedation for now, but the plan is to keep her in the induced coma to allow her brain to continue healing properly. We don't want to rush things and risk setbacks."

Barbara nodded, absorbing the information. "As long as it's what's best for her."

Dr. Faulkner exchanged a glance with the Internist who quickly handed him a note. "Since her pneumonia is under control, she's now stable enough to proceed with the surgery to repair her femur."

Barbara looked anxious. "Surgery? Is that safe for her now?"

"Yes," Dr. Faulkner reassured her. "We've delayed it as long as we could to give her time to recover, but the orthopedic surgeon is concerned that if we wait any longer, the injury may be harder to fix. The bones need to be set properly, and the sooner we intervene, the better her chances of regaining normal function in her leg."

Dr. Roberts nodded. "The benefits outweigh the risks. The surgery will give her the best chance at walking again."

Tom rubbed his hand over his face. "So, this surgery - it's not optional, right?"

"No," Dr. Faulkner said gently. "It's a crucial step. If we wait too long, the bones might heal improperly, and that could complicate things in the future."

Nancy, still standing quietly to the side, allowed herself a smile. This was the most optimistic update they'd heard since Linda had been admitted. "It's good news, then," she said. "She's getting stronger."

The doctors gave small, reassuring smiles. They knew better than to make promises, but they could see the relief on Nancy's face, and they shared in it, however cautiously.

"Thank you," Nancy said again, looking at each doctor in turn. "You've done so much for her. I really appreciate it."

Barbara reaffirmed Nancy's gratitude; her voice was softer. "We're grateful to all of you. Just knowing she's improving is more than we could have hoped for."

Tom nodded in agreement, though his expression remained guarded. He didn't want to get his hopes up just yet. There had been too many uncertainties in the past few days, and he wasn't ready to let his guard down. But even he had to admit that things were looking better.

"Her improvement is a team effort," Dr. Faulkner said, smiling briefly. "We'll continue to monitor her closely. The orthopedic surgeon will begin preparing for the surgery later today."

With that, the doctors turned to leave.

Nancy checked her watch again. It was time for her to leave. She walked over to Barbara. "I need to get going. I'll stop by again tomorrow morning, okay?"

Barbara smiled up at her. "Thank you, Nancy. I don't know what we'd do without you."

Nancy shook her head. "You'd manage just fine. You always do."

Tom gave her a small nod of appreciation, and she returned it. They weren't exactly close, but Nancy knew how deeply he cared about Linda, even if he struggled to show it.

With a final wave, Nancy left the room, the sound of her footsteps fading down the hallway.

Barbara and Tom sat in silence for a moment, processing everything they had heard.

"I guess we should be thankful," Barbara said softly. "She's come this far."

Tom grunted in agreement, his thoughts drifting back to the garage and the work piling up. But for now, his focus had to be here, with Linda.

A nurse entered the room a few minutes later, clipboard in hand. "We'll begin prepping Linda for surgery soon," she said. "It'll take a couple of hours to get everything set up. The orthopedic team will come by shortly to take her down to the operating room."

Barbara gave the nurse a tight smile. "Thank you."

The nurse nodded and left, leaving them alone with their thoughts once more.

Barbara leaned back in her chair. "I hope this surgery goes smoothly," she whispered, more to herself than to Tom.

Tom placed a hand on her shoulder, a rare moment of tenderness between them. "It will. She's tough, just like her mother."

Barbara smiled faintly, grateful for the small comfort. And with that, they waited in the quiet room, hopeful yet anxious, as preparations for the surgery began.

Chapter Thirteen:
JJ Continues to Investigate:
Dinner at Nancy's

Nancy's children were adjusting to her new schedule leaving early for work. She kissed them all goodbye and left. She wanted to get there for report.

As Nancy crossed the parking lot, the crisp morning air did little to shake the exhaustion clinging to her bones. She spotted Father Thomas unlocking his car, his shoulders heavy with fatigue. He had been a near-constant presence at the hospital, keeping vigil beside Linda when Barbara couldn't.

He glanced up as she approached, offering a tired but warm smile. She returned it with a small wave. *He's done more for the Berrys than most people would. And yet, it's never enough, is it?*

Nancy shook off the thought and quickened her pace, pushing through the ICU doors. The scent of antiseptic and coffee—burnt and bitter—filled the air. She made her way to her office, dropping her purse onto the chair before grabbing a blank sheet of paper. There was no time to settle in. Report was about to start.

The break room was already full of nurses, their voices low, a mix of exhaustion and routine familiarity in the air.

Nancy slid into an empty chair, nodding a quiet greeting. As the night shift nurse began the handover, she scribbled down notes, her pen moving in steady, practiced strokes.

When Linda's name came up, she felt herself tense.

"Her femur surgery went as expected," the night nurse reported. "Vitals are stable, but no change neurologically. Still unresponsive."

Nancy bit the inside of her cheek, her fingers tightening around her pen. *Still unresponsive.* The words echoed in her mind, colder each time. She glanced at Carol when the nurse finished speaking.

"Carol, can I talk to you for a minute?" Nancy asked, standing.

Carol nodded, tucking her notepad under her arm as they stepped aside. Nancy took a slow breath, searching for the right words.

"How did she do overnight?" she asked, keeping her voice steady.

Carol hesitated before answering, her eyes soft with understanding. "The same. No real changes. Barbara was in and out, and Father Thomas stayed with her most of the night. He barely left her side."

Nancy exhaled, her gaze drifting toward the ICU doors.

They both left the report room. Carol headed toward her patients. Nancy took a walk around the unit checking on each patient, making sure the supply room was adequately stocked, checked the med cart and the blanket warmer.

Then she went into the break room and cleaned up the area which really wasn't that messy.

Next Nancy headed for her office to start going over the papers on her desk. The phone rang. It was Mrs. Collins.

"How are you settling in?" she asked.

"So far, things are going well. I was just going to finish going over the papers you asked me to review more carefully."

"That's a good start. I know you have a lot to think about. I called to remind you of the lunch meeting in Doctors' cafeteria at noon."

"Thank you," Nancy said. "I was going to put them on my phone calendar as a pop-up reminder. I just haven't gotten to it yet."

"That's a good idea," Mrs. Collins said. "I only called so you wouldn't miss your first meeting."

"I appreciate the reminder. I wouldn't want to miss my first meeting."

"Okay, see you there." Mrs. Collins hung up.

. .
.

Meanwhile, JJ headed to Tom's garage to talk to him. Only Brian was there.

"Where's Tom? he asked.

"Still at the medical center. He should be here shortly. We fixed his wife's car. Now he can leave and she has transportation."

"What happened to her car?"

"Tom said he hit a deer or something."

"When was that?"

"The night Linda got hit by Nancy's house."

"There seems to be a lot of deer getting hit."

"Yeah, it happens." "I think Tom was pretty drunk after leaving the Roadhouse."

Just then Tom showed up in his truck.

JJ greeted him. "How's Linda doing?"

"She's stable and had her thigh bone repaired."

"I heard you hit a deer that night."

"I definitely hit something, but it ran off and I never saw it."

"What color is your wife's car?"

"Well, it was silver, but she liked the priest's car so I painted it blue for her."

I have some other places to go, but best wishes for Linda. I hope she makes a complete recovery."

"Thanks, JJ, see you around."

. .
.

JJ got into his vehicle and drove off. He headed for the Roadhouse. When he arrived, there were only two cars in the lot. He got out and walked to the door which was locked. He knocked loudly several times.

Finally, he heard someone shout," We're not open until 5."

"Police he hollered back."

The door opened and the owner stepped out. "What can I do for you?"

"I'd like to ask you a few questions.".

"Okay, come on in,"

They sat at one of the clean tables. "Were you here Tuesday night?" JJ asked.

I'm here almost every night and I think I was here Tuesday," he answered.

"Was Tom Berry here?"

"I don't know about Tuesday but there was a group of guys playing cards and drinking one night. Even Father Thomas was here. He wasn't gambling but he was putting back the Scotch like there was no tomorrow."

"Well, it wasn't Wednesday, Thursday, or Friday— Saturday and Sunday are accounted for too. So, do you think it was Monday or Tuesday?"

The bartender leaned against the counter, rubbing his chin in thought. "Well, based on what you just said, it must've been Tuesday. Monday was slow, hardly anyone came in."

JJ nodded, his gaze steady. "Do you remember how much he had to drink?" He held up a hand before the bartender could get defensive. "I'm not here to bust you for overserving. This is about an accident investigation. I just need the truth."

The bartender exhaled through his nose, crossing his arms. "In that case... I'd say most of them were pretty well tanked—including Tom. Someone even hit my sign out front when they left."

JJ's expression didn't change, but his mind started turning. *That could mean something—or nothing. But if Tom was as drunk as the others, he wouldn't have been steady behind the wheel.*

"Thanks for your honesty. That could be helpful," JJ said, sliding a business card across the bar. "If you could jot down the names of the guys who were here that night, that'd help too. Doesn't have to be perfect—just whoever you remember."

The bartender picked up the card, glancing at it.

"When you're done with the list, call me," JJ continued. "I'll have a patrolman come by to pick it up. If we need more names, I'll track them down from there." He tapped the card. "The second number is my private line. Call that one."

The bartender gave him a slow nod. "Will do."

As JJ turned to leave, he could feel the weight of the bartender's gaze on his back. *One more piece to the puzzle,* he thought. *Now, let's see where it fits.*

．．

JJ thanked him again, got up and left. He got back in his car to go, but stopped at the sign, got out and found blue paint chips on the ground. He begged them and dated and signed the evidence bag. He put them in his car and headed for the station.

When he arrived the desk Sergeant said, "Someone named Nancy called you. She wouldn't tell me what it was about but she left her number." He handed JJ the slip of paper with the number.

JJ didn't recognize the number but he went back to his office and called it.

Nancy answered saying "Hello, this is Nancy King, Director of ICU. How may I help you?"

"No wonder I didn't recognize this number. It's your office number for your new job."

"Oh—hey, JJ." Nancy shifted the phone to her other hand, exhaling. "I'm really sorry I didn't call you back on Friday. Work was crazy, and then I spent some time with Linda. By the time I got home, I was exhausted—I completely forgot."

She sighed, rubbing her forehead. *Not exactly the best way to keep a conversation going with someone you actually like.*

"Saturday and Sunday were a blur," she continued. "I wanted to spend time with the kids, get some shopping done, tackle the mountain of laundry—oh, and actually clean the house for once." She let out a soft chuckle, though she knew she was rambling. *Just get to the point, Nancy.*

She hesitated for half a second before pushing forward.

"Anyway… I know this is super last-minute, but would you like to come over for dinner tonight?" Her pulse picked up slightly. "I figured it'd be nice to catch up—and I'd really like to see you."

"I have some reports to go over and some people to talk to. What time were you thinking?"

"Is six o'clock too early?"

"No, I think I can wrap it up by then. What can I bring?"

"Don't laugh. Bring some soda for the kids. I don't let them have it often and you will be their hero."

. .
.

JJ picked up the accident file. The blood matched Linda's type. The blue paint chips came from a Chevrolet. The silver chips also came from a Chevrolet. This was confusing because Nancy's car was silver and Barbara's car had been silver but Tom had painted it and it was unlikely he had used Chevy paint. Something to ask him about later. The fibers matched Linda's clothing. Then he remembered the new chips he had found at the damaged sign.

He took the new chips to the Desk Sergeant and asked him to get them sent to the State Police for analysis.

Nancy left work a little early. She had decided to make dinner simple. Something the kids would like and hopefully JJ too. She bought bowtie pasta, ground turkey, garlic bread, and sauce and salad fixings. When she got home the kids were already there.

"No practices today?" she asked.

"No, we had a fake bomb threat at the end of the day. They sent us and kids from the other schools home early," said Bill.

"We are having company for dinner so I would like some help cleaning up the kitchen and setting the table while I cook. Debbie, you can make the salad."

"Who is coming to dinner?" Bill asked.

"Detective Jason," she replied.

"Why?" they all asked.

"Because I invited him. Now get to work."

While Bill cleaned things up Bob set the table. Nancy added spices and bread crumbs to the ground turkey and cooked them. When they were ready, she heated the sauce and put the meatballs in to simmer in the sauce. She heated a pan of water to cook the bowtie pasta but waited to do that just before six. Then she put the garlic bread in the oven.

Debbie finished the salad and put it in the refrigerator.

"Thank you all for your help. I couldn't have done it by myself. As a reward, you can watch TV and do your homework after dinner."

It didn't take them 30 seconds to get to the family room and turn on the TV.

At 5:45 she put the pasta on to cook.

. .
.

It was getting late but just as JJ was leaving the owner of the Roadhouse called to say he had a list for him. JJ asked the Desk Sergeant to send a patrolman to the Roadhouse to pick up the list.

He left the police station and went home to change his clothes. On the way, he stopped at the grocery store and picked up a six-pack of Coke and a few candy bars. He finally got home, washed up, changed his clothes and headed for Nancy's house. He figured he'd be 5-10 minutes late.

When he arrived, he had the soda in his hand but kept the candy bars in his jacket pocket, waiting to see how things went.

Nancy greeted him warmly and told the kids it was time for dinner. They entered the kitchen slowly not looking at JJ.

"You remember Detective Jason. He's the one who questioned you about the phone."

They all nodded.

"Well, he's not here to question you tonight. He is here to have dinner with us as he helped me get my bag phone back."

At that moment Cody came bounding out and jumped all over JJ.

"Stop that jumping Cody," Linda said in a loud voice.

"It's okay," JJ said. I love dogs. I would have one if I didn't work so much. He petted the dog.

"You're the hero dog who helped Nancy find Linda; good boy."

"He is a good dog for the most part. He just gets excited when we have company."

"Come on Cody, I'll give you a treat, "said Bob. The dog immediately left JJ and ran to Bob.

"Okay," said Nancy. "Enough excitement."

JJ said, "I brought you all a present your mother said you would like," as he held out the soda.

"Can we have it with dinner?" they chorused.

"Yes. Debbie, you get the salad and dressing and I will put the pasta and meatballs with sauce on the table. You can all start serving yourselves while I slice the garlic bread."

Bill grabbed a bottle opener and began opening and pouring the soda into glasses.

The children were silent as they ate until JJ started asking about basketball, soccer and gymnastics. Then they opened up slowly and finally hardly anyone could get a word in. JJ was an expert in getting people to talk – it was part of his job.

After dinner, JJ offered to help clean up.

"Absolutely not," said Nancy. "You are a guest, but you could see if anyone needs help with their homework."

. .
.

JJ went into the family room. Debbie was on the couch. Bill was sitting at a small desk. Bob had papers spread all over the rug.

"Does anyone need help with their homework?"

"No", they all responded.

"Well, I have another surprise for you. Desert." He pulled three candy bars out of his pocket.

They all jumped up and ran to him to get first pick.

"But first you have to answer two questions?"

"Did your mother hit a deer?"

"Is this a trick question," Bill asked. "You know she hit a deer."

"Okay, but when did it happen?"

"About 2 to 3 weeks ago," answered Debbie.

"That's 2 questions," said Bob.

"Indeed, it is," said JJ as he handed over the candy bars.

Munching on their candy bars, the kids went back to their homework. JJ wandered back to the kitchen.

"Are you sure there is nothing I can help you with?"

"Everything is done. I'm just waiting for the leftovers to cool down before I put them in the refrigerator."

"How is the hit-and-run case going?"

"I have a list of possible suspects that should be on my desk tomorrow."

"I only ask because I feel like I am a suspect."

"Well, you have been cleared by me."

"I haven't been cleared by everyone. When I visit Linda and Tom is there, he looks at me in a menacing way and he acts like I might be the one who hit Linda."

"Tom looks menacing to everyone. That's just Tom."

"Can I get a look at that list? I know more people in Warren than you do."

"I can't give it to you, but if you go to the Roadhouse the owner can tell you who is on the list."

Okay, I understand."

You know it's getting late and we both have work tomorrow. Thank you for a wonderful dinner and a chance to meet your kids under less stressful circumstances. I think I'd better get going."

I wanted to spend more time with you, but you're right. "

Chapter Fourteen:
Promising Progress

D r. Roberts, the orthopedic surgeon, stood by the lightboard in Linda's ICU room, his sharp eyes scanning the latest postoperative X-ray. The black-and-white image cast a glow over his face as he traced the outline of the metal rod and screws now holding her shattered femur together. A satisfied smile tugged at his lips.

"Looks good," he murmured, stepping back. Relief flickered in his chest—this had been a tricky repair, but everything was holding in place.

Dr. Faulkner, the pulmonologist, glanced up from his notes and took a closer look at the X-ray. "That fracture was a mess," he admitted. "But the alignment looks solid. No displacement, no sign of infection. Good work."

Roberts gave a modest shrug. "It's a team effort. Now, we wait. The body has to do its part."

From the corner of the room, Barbara sat up straighter, her hands clasped tightly in her lap. Hope shimmered in her tired eyes. "So… does that mean she'll walk again?"

Roberts turned toward her with a reassuring smile. "Yes, Mrs. Berry, though it will take time.

We'll need physical therapy once she's stable enough, but she has a very good chance of regaining full mobility. The surgery went as well as we could've hoped."

Barbara nodded; relief visible in her expression. "Thank you, Doctor. That's good to hear."

Tom, standing by the window, gave a brief nod at the news.

"Best news so far," he said.

Dr. Faulkner looked at her chest x-ray and said," Her lungs are fully expanded. I think we can take the chest tube out now. Roberts, can you give me a hand?"

"Sure".

Dr. Faulkner hailed a nurse and asked her to bring the equipment he needed.

She returned with everything, but asked, "Is there anything else you need?"

Dr. Faulkner said, "No, thanks."

Dr. Faulkner got down on one knee and removed the tape around the tube. Dr. Roberts handed him the scissors and he cut the sutures holding the tube in.

"Ready," he asked Dr. Roberts?

Dr. Roberts nodded.

Dr. Faulkner pulled the tube out as gently as possible and Dr. Roberts quickly covered the opening with a special bandage holding it firmly in place while Dr. Faulkner taped it securely.

"That looks great," said Dr. Roberts.

Dr. Patel, not to be ignored, held a tablet displaying the latest cranial CT scan, cleared his throat. "Speaking of recovery, I've reviewed Linda's CT scan from this morning, and there are encouraging signs.

The intracranial bleeding is subsiding, and the brain swelling has gone down considerably."

Tom's eyes widened with excitement. "Does that mean she's getting better?"

"Yes," Patel replied. "But slowly. The injury was severe, and we have to be patient. She's still in the induced coma to protect her brain and give it time to heal properly."

Barbara frowned slightly, worry still lingering on her face. "How long will she need to stay in the coma?"

Patel placed the tablet on a table close by. "It depends. We'll continue to monitor her closely but for now, keeping her in the coma is the best course of action. We'll reassess every day."

Chapter Fifteen:
Road House and Other Interviews

JJ went to the police station. He asked the Desk Sergeant for the list the owner of the Roadhouse sent. The sergeant shuffled through some papers and finally came up with it.

"Can you make a copy of this for me?"

"Sure," the sergeant said. He made a copy and handed it to JJ.

"I will find Mike's number. Can you find all the others and if they aren't home the best number to reach them at?"

JJ turned and headed to his office. He decided to call rather than find each man. It would be less intimidating and save a lot of time.

He found Mike's number, called and a woman answered.

"Hello," he said "this is Detective Jame Jason I am trying to get in touch with Mike."

"Nothing serious, just an accident he might have witnessed. Do you have a number where I can reach him?"

"Just a moment, he's at work," she replied.

"It's 542-8175".

"Thank you, have a nice day," he said and hung up the phone.

JJ called the number she had given him. It was answered on the 5th ring.

"Mike's Hardware, how can I help you?"

"Could I speak to Mike?"

"Speaking."

"Mike, this is Detective James Jason."

"Hi JJ, what can I do for you?"

"You played cards at the Roadhouse last Tuesday,"

"Yes.".

"Can you remember who was there?"

"Let me see, there was Paul on my left, Roy on my right, Tom was there and some new guy Ron."

"How about David and Brian?"

"Oh yeah, they were there."

"Anyone else?"

"Not that I can think of off the top of my head."

"Well, if you think of anyone else, give me a call. And what's Ron's last name?"

"I don't know, but he bought the Clark's place."

"How drunk was everyone?"

"Where is this going?"

'I'll ask the questions, but it's about an accident."

"We were all pretty well buzzed, but I didn't have or see an accident."

"How about Tom?"

"You already know he's got a problem with alcohol and he was probably the worst, but we drove home different ways."

"Thanks for your help. If you think of anyone else being there, please give me a call."

JJ went to the front desk.

"Do you have those numbers for me, he asked the Desk Sergeant."

"I did the best I could, but I don't know this Ron guy. He's new in town."

"That's okay, give me what you've got."

JJ went back to his office.

Next, he called Paul. No answer.

Then he tried Roy.

"Jack's Video, how can I help you?"

Does Roy work for you?"

"Yes."

"Is he around?"

"Is this JJ?"

"Yes.".

"Is Roy in trouble?"

"No, I just have a few questions for him."

"Okay, I'll get him."

After about 3 minutes, Roy got on the phone.

"What's up, JJ?"

"You played cards at the Roadhouse last Tuesday?"

"Yes.".

"Can you remember who was there?"

"Let me see, there was Paul, David, Mike, Brian, Tom and there was a new guy, Ron."

"Anyone else?"

"Not that I can think of."

"How drunk was everyone?"

"We were all a little tipsy."

"How about Tom?"

"As usual, he was way over the limit. He's almost always the last to leave."

"Well, if you remember anyone else there, let me know."

"Will do," he said and hung up.

. .
.

JJ finished writing up his notes and decided Paul wouldn't call until after work. He decided to take a ride out to the Clark's place to see if he could find Ron.

When he arrived, there was a car in the driveway slightly beaten up.

He knocked on the door and an average-sized man with light brown hair answered the door.

"Can I help you?"

"Hi, I'm Detective Jason James. I'd like to ask you a few questions."

"Come on in."

They sat in a sparsely furnished kitchen.

"I just moved in and I don't have everything moved or unpacked."

"First, do you have I.D.?"

Ron took out his wallet and showed him his driver's license. His name was Ron Whitlow and he still had a Gardner address on his license."
"If you're planning on living here you need to get your license changed."

"I will as soon as things settle down a little. I'm starting work at the cement plant next week."

"You played cards with a group of men at the Roadhouse last Tuesday?"

"Yes, trying to get to know some people here."

"Do you know the names of the men you sat with?"

"There was a David, a Tom and a Brian. I can't remember the others' names,"

"Was there anyone else?"

Now that you mention it there was a priest there. I forget his name, but he wasn't gambling. He said he likes to hang out with his parishioners socially from time to time. He was putting down the Scotch pretty good though."

"Were the other men pretty drunk?"

"They weren't holding back, but I left first after they cleaned me out. I don't know what happened after I left."

"I notice your car is a little beaten up in the front."

"Yeah, some guy ran a red light and I couldn't stop fast enough. Still waiting for the insurance check."

"Where and when was that?"

"In Gardner, about a week ago, when I was moving. I had a U-Haul so I couldn't stop as fast."

JJ made a note to check that out.

"Thank you for your help," said JJ as he got up to leave."

"Anytime," said Ron as he held out his hand to shake.

JJ shook his hand and left.

. .
.

Now he thought I'll go talk to Barbara. He headed for Linda's house, knowing she would be there looking after her kids. When he arrived, Barbara's car and Tom's truck were both there. He got out, walked to the door and knocked.

"Come in," someone yelled.

He opened the door and saw Barbara cooking dinner.

"Is Tom here too? I'd like to ask you some questions."

"He's watching a movie with the kids"

"Tom," she called, "can you come out here for a minute?"

Tom entered the kitchen with a look of surprise when he saw JJ standing there.

"Can we sit down? I'd like to ask you some questions about Linda."

As they sat down at the table, Tom asked, "What about her?"

"You're both here so who is staying with her, Nancy?"

"No, Father Tomas relieved me. He stays with her most nights," said Tom.

"Do you know anyone who could purposefully do this to your daughter?"

Barbara spoke first. When it first happened, I thought maybe Nancy did it accidentally. And she's been so helpful I thought it might be guilt. But now I know she damaged her car before that night."

" Can either of you think of someone else who could have done it?"

Tom exhaled slowly, rubbing his chin as he thought. "The only one that comes to mind is her ex-boyfriend, Frank Burns." His voice carried a mix of frustration and regret. "He moved in with her when she lost her job and was living on welfare. At first, she really believed in him. She kept pushing him to find work, but… I don't think he ever tried all that hard."

He shook his head, recalling the slow unraveling of their relationship. "Then she got the new job—longer commute, longer hours—and she asked him to be home when the kids got out of school. For a while, he did. Showed up like clockwork. But then, things changed. Some days he was there, some days he wasn't. He always had an excuse—said he was out looking for work, but somehow, a job never materialized."

Tom's jaw tightened. "Eventually, she'd had enough. She kicked him out. Asked her mother to help instead." His voice dropped slightly, his expression unreadable. "I don't think Frank ever really let that go."

"Do you know where he is living now?" asked JJ.

"No, but if you ask around, someone will know," said Tom.

JJ made a note to find Frank,

"Thank you for your help. If you think of anyone else, please let me know."

"We will," said Barbara.

. .
.

JJ left for home. When he arrived, he heard the phone ringing. He didn't quite make it but Paul left a message he was home now.

JJ called Paul back.

Paul answered almost immediately.

JJ said," This is Detective James Jason calling."

"About what?" he asked.

"An accident."

He went through all the questions he had asked the others, but when he got to the drinking part, Paul told him Tom was really drunk.

"I left just before Tom and I heard a crash. I looked back and Tom had hit the Roadhouse sign. Is that the accident you're talking about?"

"Not exactly, but you have been helpful. Thanks for the information. And by the way, do you know Frank Burns?"

"Yes, he used to live with Linda."

"Do you know where he lives now?"

I heard he moved in with some chick in the trailer park.

. .
.

JJ grabbed his jacket and headed for the mobile home park. He stopped at the office and talked to the manager.

"Did a man named Frank move in here?" he asked.

"There is a new guy supposedly *visiting* Wendy, or so they say. We'll see."

"They are in number 44."

JJ got back in his car and searched for 44. He finally found it, got out and knocked on the door.

A woman answered the door.

"I'm Detective Jason James. he showed her his badge, and I am looking for Frank Burns."

"There's a cop here to see you, Frank," she said in a slightly louder voice.

She stepped aside as an average-sized man with light brown hair came to the door.

"Are you Frank Burns?" JJ asked.

"Yes."

You weren't at last Tuesday's poker game at the Roadhouse were you?" JJ asked.

"No, my buddies and me took our bikes up to Bangor to watch the demolition derby."

"Can you give me their names and phone numbers to verify this?"

Frank took out his phone and read off some names and numbers as JJ jotted them down on his pad.

"Thanks for your help," he said.

The door closed.

Chapter Sixteen:
Off the Ventilator

D r. Faulkner sat at his desk, sifting through the last of the paperwork for the day. His pen scratched the surface of his notes, and he paused occasionally to adjust his reading glasses, glancing at the clock with a small smile. It was Wednesday, a day he always looked forward to for more than just the end of his shift. His wife had a tradition of making his favorite meal on Wednesdays - an aromatic, slow-cooked lamb roast that filled their house with warmth and comfort the moment he walked in. He closed his file, leaned back, and allowed himself a moment to think of the evening ahead. But before he could let his thoughts drift too far, he remembered he had one last patient to see: Linda.

Linda had been his patient for a while now. He and the team were invested in her recovery. Her case was severe, but Dr. Faulkner had started noticing some signs of improvement. He wasn't about to leave the medical center without one last check on her, especially since her lung function had been progressing well. Picking up his office phone, he dialed the nursing station, leaning back in his chair as he waited for someone to answer.

"Yes, Dr. Faulkner," a voice replied on the other end.

"Could you meet me outside Linda's ICU room?" he asked. "I'd like to review her charts and maybe see if we can move forward with extubating her."

"Yes, Doctor. I'll be there shortly," the nurse replied.

With a nod to himself, he set the phone down, gathered his things, and walked out of his office, shutting the door behind him. As he made his way down the brightly lit corridor, he spotted the nurse coming from the opposite direction, her arms filled with Linda's chart and a few necessary supplies.

"Good evening, Doctor," she greeted him with a warm smile.

"Good evening. Let's see how our patient is doing," Dr. Faulkner said, falling into step beside her as they made their way down the hushed corridor toward the ICU. The rhythmic beeping of monitors grew louder with each step, blending with the faint antiseptic scent that lingered in the air. Overhead, the fluorescent lights flickered ever so slightly, casting long, sterile shadows along the walls.

As they stepped into Linda's room, Dr. Faulkner's gaze immediately landed on a figure seated across from the bed. His head was bowed, his fingers resting lightly on the pages of a small, well-worn pamphlet. The dim glow of the bedside monitor illuminated his face—lined with quiet contemplation.

Father Thomas.

The priest, known for his gentle spirit and unwavering dedication to his congregation, looked up at their arrival. His warm eyes softened further, and a slow smile spread across his face. He rose from his chair, smoothing the front of his cassock as he extended a hand.

"Dr. Faulkner," he greeted warmly. "It's been too long, my friend."

Dr. Faulkner's eyes lit up with recognition. "Father Thomas! It's good to see you," he replied, extending a hand. The priest took it in both of his, patting it warmly. The two shared a brief moment of familiarity, bridging the gap of years.

"Bless you for taking care of Linda," Father Thomas said sincerely, a gleam of gratitude in his eyes. "She's been through so much. I've been praying for her recovery."

Dr. Faulkner nodded, touched by the priest's words. "Thank you, Father. I know she has a strong support system, and that makes all the difference." He hesitated a moment, then smiled sheepishly as Father Thomas fixed him with a knowing look.

"You haven't been to church in ages, Dr. Faulkner," Father Thomas observed, his eyes shifting with gentle reproach. "I hope it's not because you've forgotten us."

Dr. Faulkner chuckled, rubbing the back of his neck. "Not forgotten, Father. Can't forget. I've just been busy. You know how it is. Work keeps me here most of the time."

Father Thomas nodded, understanding but undeterred. "Well, make time when you can. We miss seeing you around."

Before Dr. Faulkner could respond, the nurse had pulled out Linda's chart, flipping it open for the doctor to review. He glanced over the latest readings and test results, nodding as he absorbed the information. Everything seemed to indicate progress.

"Her lungs are recovering amazingly," Dr. Faulkner remarked, facing Father Thomas. He looked up at Father

Thomas, who was watching him intently. "I think we can take her off the ventilator today. It's a promising step forward."

Father Thomas clasped his hands together in obvious joy. "That's wonderful news. God is good," he murmured, his voice cheerful.

"Let's start setting her up." he said looking at the nurse. We can turn off the ventilator and extubate her now."

The nurse positioned herself by Linda's bedside, carefully raising the bed into a more upright position as Dr. Faulkner directed her. He moved to the ventilator, his fingers flying over the buttons as he prepared to power it down. He'd done this countless times before, but there was something about each extubation that carried a particular weight - a symbolic moment when the patient's body began to reclaim its autonomy.

"Alright," Dr. Faulkner said, his voice low but confident. He powered down the ventilator, and the sound that had been filling the room with a steady rhythm ceased. For a moment, all eyes were on Linda as they waited, watching the slight rise and fall of her chest, hoping it would continue steadily.

Dr. Faulkner leaned in, observing her closely, his eyes flicking between her chest movements and the monitor displaying her respiratory rate. Each breath was shallow, almost tentative, as though her body was unsure of its own strength. But she was breathing on her own, a victory, however small.

"It's not as deep as we'd like," Dr. Faulkner said, straightening up. "But it's expected, given that her chest is still frail from the broken ribs. We'll keep her on oxygen for now to support her breathing."

The nurse stepped forward with the materials needed for extubation. Dr. Faulkner suctioned her endotracheal tube one last time, cut the tape holding the tube in and then watched for her to exhale, slipping the tube out with a practiced hand. He watched her for another moment, his expression a mix of pride and vigilance, as her body adjusted to this new phase of her recovery.

Father Thomas, who had been standing quietly by, watching each step with patience and in awe, finally spoke up, his voice filled with cheer. "It's remarkable, Doctor. The way you all work together to heal and mend."

Dr. Faulkner offered a small, humble smile. "It's a team effort," he replied. "The human body is capable of incredible things, given the right support."

Father Thomas nodded; his eyes warm. "Linda's journey is a testament to that. And to the power of faith."

Dr. Faulkner glanced over at Father Thomas, appreciating the priest's unwavering belief. Though he wasn't particularly religious himself, he respected the strength that faith seemed to give people. He looked back at Linda, her face peaceful, her breathing even, and he felt a quiet sense of fulfillment.

"Do you think she's out of the woods?" Father Thomas asked quietly, his gaze still fixed on Linda.

"She's making progress," Dr. Faulkner replied cautiously. "Her body is healing, and so far her recovery is commendable. At this rate, she'll be out of the ICU in no time."

Father Thomas nodded, seeming to absorb this, and he bowed his head, murmuring a quiet prayer under his breath. Dr. Faulkner allowed him the moment.

After a few minutes, Dr. Faulkner turned to the nurse. "Let's keep monitoring her oxygen levels and adjust as needed. For now, we'll keep it at 4 liters per minute. I'll have someone check on her again in a few hours."

The nurse nodded, making a note in Linda's chart, her movements efficient but gentle as she adjusted Linda's oxygen tube. Dr. Faulkner watched as the nurse stepped back, her eyes trained on the monitors that tracked Linda's every breath.

Satisfied that everything was in order, Dr. Faulkner looked back at Father Thomas. "Thank you for being here for her," he said, his voice warm. "I know it must mean a lot to her, even if she can't express it right now."

Father Thomas smiled; his face softened by compassion. "Being here for others, whether in spirit or body is what matters most. It's something we all need from time to time."

Dr. Faulkner nodded, feeling a pang of understanding. He knew that, despite the clinical, scientific nature of his work, there was an element of healing that went beyond medicine. A kind of support that came from the presence of others, from the reassurance of knowing that someone cared.

As they made their way toward the door, Father Thomas placed a hand on Dr. Faulkner's shoulder. "We'd love to see you in church again soon," he said, his voice light but hopeful

Dr. Faulkner offered a small, sheepish smile. "I'll try to make it, Father."

Father Thomas's eyes twinkled with warmth. "We'll keep a seat ready for you."

With a final nod, Dr. Faulkner stepped out of the room, leaving Linda in the capable hands of the nurse and under the gentle gaze of Father Thomas. Walking down the hallway, he felt a quiet sense of fulfillment, his mind lingering on the journey Linda was making back to health. With each step, he let himself believe that, despite the challenges ahead, recovery was possible. As he walked back to his office to finish up and head home, his mind drifted back to the meal waiting for him at home.

Chapter Seventeen:
Nancy Calls JJ

The phone was ringing and JJ reluctantly answered it. He had been talking all day and he was tired.

"Hello," he said.

"Hi, said Nancy. I hope I'm not bothering you."

"You're never a bother, what's up?"

"I've been thinking

"Uh oh," he interrupted.

"Very funny, now can I finish?"

"Please go on."

"How many suspects do you have left?"

"Well, I have cleared all the men at the Roadhouse who were drinking together. I have two other suspects that appear to have solid alibis, but I need to check them out. Why?"

"I know it's a long shot but Father Thomas had something wrong with his car and he took it all the way to the dealership in Augusta. That seems suspicious to me. Could you spray some of that stuff under his car to check for blood?"

"You mean Luminol?"

"Yes. He's parked at the medical center right now and would never know you did it."

"Only for you would I do this and you can't tell anyone."

"I won't."

"Okay, I'll do it right now and call you back."

"Thank you for indulging me. Talk to you later".

JJ hung up the phone and went to the police station. He grabbed a can of Luminal and headed out for the medical center.

There were very few cars in the parking lot so it was easy to find Father Thomas' car. He sprayed the Luminol under the front and there was no blood. He tried underneath the middle and back with the same results.

He drove home keeping the Luminol and called Nancy back.

"Hello," she said.

"I'm sorry but I practically sprayed the whole car and there was no sign of blood."

"Well, thank you," she said, sounding disappointed.

"It was a good idea. I'm sorry it didn't work out. Why don't I take you to dinner this weekend to reward your idea and cheer you up from your disappointment?"

" You don't have to do that. I think Billy might have a basketball game. Raincheck?"

"Definitely. Unless I can go to his game."

"I will let you know the details if you're serious."

"Thanks, I am. Talk to you later."

Chapter Eighteen:
Weaning off the Sedation

Then he nodded politely to Barbara and Tom. "Good morning Mr. and Mrs. Berry." Barbara and Tom returned the greetings, and the doctors moved further into the room, focusing their attention on Linda. Dr. Faulkner took the lead, looking directly at Barbara as he began to explain Linda's condition.

"Good morning, Nancy," Dr. Faulkner greeted. "You're in early to see her today. I'm sure your shift doesn't start till 8 am."

"I wanted to update you on what we did last night," he began. "Linda's lungs have shown significant improvement, which is why we felt confident enough to intubate her. She's breathing on her own now, without the support of the ventilator. Her body seems to be handling it well."

Barbara's eyes sparkled with relief, and she exchanged a hopeful glance with Tom. "That's such wonderful news, Dr. Faulkner. We've been praying for this day."

Dr. Faulkner gave a small nod, with a bit of pride in his expression. "It's a testament to her strength and to the care she's been receiving," he replied. "She'll still need oxygen support for a while, but this is a huge step forward."

Dr. Patel stood beside Linda, his expression calm but focused. "I want to assess her current neurological state," he said, reaching into his pocket for the tools he always carried for quick examinations.

With practiced precision, he gently lifted one of Linda's eyelids, shining a penlight into her pupil. The small beam reflected in her eye, and he watched closely, waiting. A flicker. A response. He gave a small nod of approval.

He moved on, testing her reflexes—each assessment measured, each result carefully noted. With every response, his confidence grew. "Linda's neurological signs are showing improvement," he finally announced, his voice steady but laced with the cautious optimism of a man who had seen too many unpredictable cases.

Abigail, already anticipating his next steps, had her notepad ready, pen poised. Dr. Patel glanced at her, then back at Linda. "We'll start reducing the sedation," he continued, jotting a quick note. "Right now, she's on 216 mg of propofol. We'll lower it by 10 mg every hour."

He paused, his gaze settling on Linda's still form. "This will give her time to regain more consciousness—gradually, as her body stabilizes." His voice softened just slightly. "She'll need to be closely monitored."

Abigail nodded, scribbling down his orders while the steady beeping of the monitors filled the silence.

Dr. Patel stepped back, giving Linda one last measured look. "Let's see how she does," he murmured, more to himself than anyone else. Then, with a final glance at the team, he turned toward the door, leaving hope lingering in the sterile air.

Meanwhile, Dr. Roberts had put on a pair of sterile gloves and approached Linda's leg, where the surgical wound from her previous procedure was healing. He gently examined the area, his eyes keenly observant. After a careful inspection, he leaned back, removing his gloves and disposing of them.

"The wound is healing even better than I expected," Dr. Roberts noted, directing his comment to the group. "It's a promising sign, especially given the complexity of the surgery."

"Her chest tube site doesn't seem to be leaking. If all goes well, we'll take that dressing off tomorrow the next day," said Dr. Faulkner.

Nurse Abigail quickly recorded the findings in Linda's chart, making note of each doctor's assessment and orders. The room was filled with a quiet feeling of optimism as the medical team observed Linda's progress.

Dr. Patel looked over at Barbara and Tom with a reassuring smile. "I'll come back to check on her later in a few hours," he said. "I want to see how she's handling the reduced sedation. She should be off it by tomorrow morning."

Dr. Faulkner and Dr. Roberts nodded in agreement, echoing their commitment to closely watch Linda's progress. Each of them understood the delicate balance required in managing her recovery, and they were dedicated to guiding her safely through each stage.

The doctors and Abigail finished their work, and each exchanged kind farewells with Barbara, Tom, and Nancy as they prepared to leave the room. Dr. Patel offered a final word of encouragement. "We'll be here every step of the way. She's doing incredibly well, thanks to all of you being here too."

After they left, Nancy glanced at her watch and sighed, a touch of reluctance in her eyes. "I should probably head out too," she said, standing and gathering her things. "Duty calls."

Barbara gave her a warm smile. "We're so grateful to have you here, Nancy. Take care of yourself, and have a lovely day at work."

Nancy smiled, feeling the warmth of their gratitude. "It's my pleasure. I'll be back in the morning."

As Nancy left the room, Barbara turned to Tom, her eyes soft with emotion. "I can't wait for Linda to wake up," she exclaimed. "I miss talking to her, hearing her voice. It feels like it's been so long."

"It won't be long now," Tom said, his voice steady with hope. "She's coming back to us."

They stood together in quiet anticipation.

Evenings at the medical center were usually quiet, the hum of monitors and the occasional footsteps of nurses the only sounds filling the dimly lit halls. As the sun dipped below the horizon, a golden glow cast long shadows through the windows, softening the sterile edges of the ward.

It had been a long day for everyone involved in Linda's care. The medical team had taken another step forward, gradually decreasing her sedation—a delicate but significant move in her recovery. Yet, Linda remained still, caught in that fragile space between deep rest and wakefulness, her body healing in its own time.

When Father Thomas arrived, Barbara felt an immediate sense of relief. She managed a tired but genuine smile as he stepped into the room. "Thank you again for being here," she said, her voice warm but edged with exhaustion. "It means a lot."

He waved a hand dismissively, his expression kind. "It's no trouble at all. She shouldn't be alone."

Barbara exhaled, nodding. She and Tom had to leave for the evening—there were children to tend to, a home that needed them, and a delicate balance to maintain between being here for Linda and keeping life moving outside these hospital walls.

She lingered momentarily at Linda's bedside, brushing a hand over her daughter's fingers. "I'll be back first thing in the morning," she whispered, more to herself than anyone else.

With one last grateful glance at Father Thomas, she and Tom stepped out of the room, leaving behind the rhythmic beeping of the monitors and the steady presence of the man who had become a source of quiet comfort.

Tom had taken a brief break earlier in the day, retreating to his garage for a few hours to check in on work. It was a rare chance for him to reset.

As the evening wore on, the nurse on duty, who had taken over from Abigail, noticed a shift in Linda's vitals. Her heart rate had begun to climb steadily, her blood pressure spiking in response. Concerned, the nurse didn't hesitate; she immediately paged Dr. Patel, who arrived in short order, his expression was calm as he approached Linda's bed.

Dr. Patel conducted a quick assessment, his eyes focused on the monitors and Linda herself, carefully observing the rhythm of her breathing and the subtle involuntary movements of her body. He took note of the medications currently administered, his mind running through possible reasons for the sudden shift in her condition.

After a moment's thought, he pulled out a small vial from his kit, administering an additional dose to help stabilize her heart rate and ease her blood pressure back into a safer range.

Father Thomas was beside Linda in his usual seat, watching the doctor keenly as he worked. He was eager to know what was going on.

Dr. Patel caught his eye and offered a reassuring nod. "It's nothing out of the ordinary," he explained, gesturing to the heart monitor, which now displayed a more regular rhythm. "When patients are taken off sedation, it's common for the body to go through an adjustment phase. The nervous system starts to 'wake up,' so to speak, which can lead to fluctuations like these."

Father Thomas nodded, listening intently. He glanced at Linda, whose face appeared peaceful but somewhat distant as if caught in a world beyond their reach. "You're sure she's going to be okay, though?" he asked, a slight tremor in his voice betraying his worry.

Dr. Patel's gaze softened. "Yes, Father, these things are expected and manageable," he assured him. "In fact, earlier, when you weren't here, she had a similar episode. Linda experienced some jerky movements - likely a seizure or something similar. But we administered an anticonvulsant, and that resolved it."

Father's face tightened, his usual calm demeanor faltering under the weight of his anxiety. The idea of Linda experiencing seizures or other complications was unsettling, a reminder of just how delicate her condition truly was. "So... what does this mean for her recovery? I mean, is this going to set her back?"

Dr. Patel placed a reassuring hand on Father's shoulder. "I know it's difficult, but try not to worry too much," he said gently. "These reactions are normal given the trauma her body has been through. The fact that she's responding to treatment and that her heart and lungs are strong enough to be off sedation is a very good sign. We'll address each issue as it arises and we will keep a close watch on her progress."

Father Thomas released a long, shaky breath, nodding slowly as he absorbed the doctor's words. The tension in his shoulders seemed to ease just a fraction, and he managed a faint smile, grateful for Dr. Patel's steady reassurance.

"Thank you, Doctor," he said. "I appreciate you being so thorough."

Dr. Patel returned the smile, his voice steady with reassurance. "It's my pleasure, Father. Just remember, recovery is rarely a straight line. There will be setbacks, but we're here to navigate them together."

With a final nod, the doctor turned and stepped out, his footsteps fading into the quiet hallway.

Left alone in the dim room, Father Thomas exhaled slowly, the weight of the day settling onto his shoulders. The steady hum of machines filled the silence, a rhythmic reminder of the fragile line between life and uncertainty. He sank into the chair beside Linda's bed, rubbing his temples as his thoughts drifted.

It had been a long day. A long week. He had seen miracles before—moments where faith and medicine intertwined, where the impossible bent just enough to let hope in. But he had also seen the other side, the cruel unpredictability of fate.

His gaze dropped to the floor, his fingers tightening around the worn edges of the prayer book in his lap.

Is she hearing us, Lord? Does she know we're here?

He leaned forward, resting his arms on the bed rail. "You're not alone, Linda," he murmured, his voice barely above a whisper. "We're all waiting for you."

And so, he remained, a quiet sentinel in the stillness, as the night stretched on.

. .
.

At home, Tom's mind shifted to his garage, the place that had become a kind of sanctuary for him over the years. It was more than just a place of work; it was a space where he could lose himself. But lately, he'd barely had time to focus on the business, juggling his responsibilities there with his role at the medical center.

From there, his thoughts drifted to the end of the day, when he would often unwind with a drink or two. A part of him craved that familiar warmth, the way it softened the edges of his worries and allowed him to let go, if only briefly.

But as he sat there, another memory surfaced - one that sent a chill down his spine. It was the night of the accident, a night that had preserved itself in his mind. He remembered the jolt, the sickening sound, and the shock that had run through him when he realized he'd hit something. He hadn't allowed himself to dwell on that night in detail, too afraid of what he might uncover if he let himself think about it for too long.

Chapter Nineteen:
Linda Wakes UP

The next morning, Barbara and Tom made their way to the medical center, exhaustion pressing down on Barbara like a weight she couldn't shake. The previous evening had been overwhelming—tidying up after the children's chaos, making sure dinner was on the table, ensuring everything at home was in order. But despite her fatigue, her mind had been elsewhere.

Now, as she walked down the familiar ICU corridor, her heart pounded with anticipation. Linda's sedation had been nearly discontinued. Any moment now, she could wake up.

"Please, let today be the day."

She exhaled sharply, barely noticing Father Thomas until they stepped into the room. He was seated beside Linda, his head bowed, whispering a final prayer. The soft hum of monitors filled the silence, their rhythmic beeping a steady reminder of the fragile balance Linda lingered in.

Barbara set her things down and leaned forward. "How did she do through the night?"

Father Thomas straightened, rubbing his eyes as if pulling himself fully into wakefulness. "Oh, Linda... Yes, she... she did great. She's fine." His voice wavered slightly, betraying his own exhaustion.

Barbara's sharp eyes studied him. He looked worn, the kind of tired that settled deep in the bones. *He must have dozed off,* she realized.

Father Thomas shifted uncomfortably, glancing at Linda's still form. He wasn't sure if anything had happened during the night, but he figured that if it had, the commotion would have jolted him awake. *Wouldn't it?*

Barbara sighed her voice soft but firm. "You should go home. Take a bath, eat something, and get some rest."

Father Thomas exhaled, stretching his stiff limbs. A faint smile touched his lips. "I didn't think I could sleep that soundly in a chair," he admitted.

Tom gave a small chuckle. "That's because you needed it."

With a grateful nod, Father Thomas took one last look at Linda, then at Barbara and Tom. "Call me if anything changes," he said before turning and walking out, his steps slow, the weight of the long night still clinging to him.

Barbara turned back to Linda, reaching for her hand, her fingers brushing gently over her daughter's cool skin. *Any minute now, baby. Just open your eyes.*

As the morning turned into afternoon, Barbara settled back in her chair beside Linda's bed, a magazine in her lap, though her attention was hardly on it. She was lost in thoughts and memories of happier times with Linda. Just as her mind drifted, she heard footsteps approaching.

"Barbara!" a warm voice called out, and she looked up to see Father Thomas entering the room, his presence bringing a sense of comfort. He had been visiting Linda regularly, offering his prayers and support to Barbara, who had found solace in his words during this trying time.

"Father Thomas, you're here early," she greeted him, smiling warmly as he approached.

He looked around, taking in the room's somber atmosphere, then gave her a reassuring smile. "You look like you could use a good laugh," he said, setting his things down.

"Oh, I wouldn't mind one," Barbara replied, smiling lightly. She put her magazine aside, grateful for the distraction. Father Thomas always knew how to lighten the mood, and soon, they were exchanging jokes, small snippets of humor to pull them out of the tension that had gripped them both.

Their laughter filled the room, lifting the heaviness that occupied the room earlier. As their laughter trailed off, a soft, unexpected sound interrupted them. Barbara's eyes widened as she heard it - a faint, almost inaudible groan.

They both turned toward Linda, their laughter fading into stunned silence as they watched her face. Her eyelids fluttered slightly, a look of distant confusion appearing in her expression. Her eyes, heavy with the fog of unconsciousness, slowly opened, blinking against the brightness in the room as if adjusting to the world around her.

"Linda..." Barbara whispered, a mixture of shock and joy coloring her voice. Her heart raced, and without thinking, she sprang from her chair, rushing to the bedside, reaching out to hold her daughter.

But as Barbara leaned closer, Linda's face contorted in fear and confusion. She looked around, her gaze darting between Barbara and Father Thomas, her eyes wide and unrecognizing. With what little strength she had, she pulled her hand back slightly, recoiling as if Barbara were a stranger.

"Linda, honey," Barbara's voice cracked as she tried to soothe her daughter. "It's me... it's your mother." Tears welled up in her eyes as she tried to make sense of Linda's reaction. She reached out again, softer this time, her hand trembling as it hovered just inches away from Linda's.

But Linda continued to shift away, her face scrunching in panic. Her movements were weak, but the emotion was unmistakable - she didn't know where she was or who was by her side. Barbara's heart shattered as she realized that her daughter was looking at her as if she were a stranger as if she had no memory of the woman standing beside her, the woman who had been praying for this moment.

Seeing Barbara's distress, Father Thomas gently took her shoulders, trying to calm her. "Barbara," he said softly, "she's just waking up. Her mind might still be confused. This is a big step, but it's going to take time."

Barbara's tears spilled over as she struggled to steady herself. She wanted so desperately to hug Linda, to assure her she was safe and loved; but the fear in Linda's eyes held her back. Just then, a nurse entered the room, closely followed by Dr. Patel. He had been alerted by the nurse's quick call.

Dr. Patel's expression turned serious as he approached Linda. "Let's give her a bit of space," he said, his voice calm, motioning for Barbara to step back. "Linda's in a fragile state right now. It's common for patients coming out of sedation to experience disorientation."

Reluctantly, Barbara allowed the nurse to guide her back, her hands falling limply at her sides as she watched Dr. Patel gently check Linda's vitals. His touch was calm, and he observed her closely as she drifted back to sleep.

As Dr. Patel finished his assessment, he turned to Barbara, offering a reassuring smile. "She's still recovering," he explained softly. "It's normal for her to feel disoriented. Her body and mind are still adjusting."

Barbara, wiping away her tears, nodded, but the pain lingered in her heart. "Thank you, Doctor," she whispered, her voice filled with despair and disappointment which she couldn't conceal.

Dr. Patel nodded, giving her a reassuring pat on the shoulder before turning to the nurse, issuing quiet instructions for Linda's continued care. Dr. Patel patted Barbara again, his arm around her shoulders, offering her the support she desperately needed. He guided her back to the armchair.

I'm exhausted," Barbara murmured, rubbing her temples. "Time to go home and get some rest."

She thanked Father Thomas once more, then stepped out into the cool night air. The parking lot was nearly empty, the glow of streetlights casting long shadows across the pavement. As she slid into her car and pulled onto the road, her mind replayed the moment over and over—the thrill of seeing Linda's eyes flutter open, the surge of relief that had turned to heartbreak when Linda's gaze remained distant, unfocused.

She hadn't recognized her.

Barbara gripped the steering wheel tighter, swallowing the lump in her throat. *She's been through so much. It's normal,* she reminded herself. *She just needs time.*

By the time she reached home, exhaustion clung to her like a heavy blanket, but she knew Tom would be waiting. As soon as she stepped inside, his anxious eyes met hers.

"She woke up," she said softly, her voice a mix of joy and sorrow.

Tom's face lit up. "She did? That's great! I need to go see her."

Barbara reached for his arm, stopping him. "She didn't recognize me, Tom." Her voice wavered, the weight of those words pressing down on her. "Dr. Patel says she needs time—to figure out where she is, what happened… what the injuries are."

Tom exhaled, his excitement dimming as reality settled in. He ran a hand through his hair, frustration evident. "But she *woke up*, Barb. That's a good sign."

She nodded. "It is. But we have to be patient. Let's give her until morning."

Tom hesitated, clearly torn, but then sighed, relenting. "Alright… first thing tomorrow."

Barbara forced a small smile, though her heart still ached. *Tomorrow.* It wasn't far, but it felt like a lifetime away.

Chapter Twenty:
Linda Wakes Up Again

In the soft glow of the early morning light, Father Thomas stood up from his chair beside Linda's bed, glancing around the quiet room. He'd stayed through the night, keeping vigil over Linda after Barbara had gone home to tend to the children and the house. The small room was a sanctuary of calm amidst the bustling corridors of the medical center, and he felt grateful for the peace it brought. Linda rested quietly, her breathing steady, her face finally showing signs of color and vitality.

Morning rounds had begun, and the rhythmic sound of footsteps echoed down the hospital hallway. A team of doctors, led by Dr. Patel, moved with quiet purpose, their white coats crisp, their faces marked with focus and fatigue in equal measure. An intern trailed behind, scribbling notes, while a nurse kept a watchful eye on the monitors as they approached Linda's room.

Inside, Father Thomas sat in his usual chair, his fingers loosely clasped in his lap. He had spent the night in quiet prayer, his presence a steady comfort even in Linda's unconscious state.

Dr. Patel stepped forward, offering a polite nod. "Good morning, Father Thomas."

The priest looked up, his warm, familiar smile barely masking his exhaustion. "Good morning, Doctor." His voice was calm, steady. He had come to know these medical professionals over the past few days, and though he didn't fully understand their world of medicine and machines, he trusted them. Their dedication was something he could believe in.

The other doctors exchanged polite acknowledgments before turning their attention to Linda. As they moved around the bed, checking vitals, reviewing charts, and murmuring quiet observations to one another, Father Thomas remained still, watching, waiting—hoping.

Dr. Roberts moved to the bedside and gently lifted the covers, checking the dressing on Linda's leg. After a moment's examination, he nodded approvingly, satisfied with the healing process. "The wound is healing well," he noted. "We've removed the dressing entirely now. There's no sign of infection, and the tissue is closing up nicely. She's making good progress."

Just as the medical team was finishing up their assessments, the door opened again, and Barbara and Tom entered the room. They looked slightly weary, but their eyes sparkled with hope as they took in the sight of the doctors.

"Good morning, everyone," Barbara said with a friendly tone as she greeted Father Thomas and the medical team. Tom nodded his own greeting, his usually guarded expression softening as he glanced at Linda.

Dr. Patel returned their greetings with a smile. "Good morning, Mr. and Mrs. Berry. We were just about to leave, but I will update you both. Linda is stable, and the wound is healing beautifully."

"Thank you, Doctor," Barbara replied gratefully. Her eyes flickered over to Linda, noticing her daughter's face seemed less pale, her cheeks showing a faint flush that hadn't been there before.

"We're all very hopeful," he said kindly. "Please be sure to let the nurse know to page me once Linda wakes up again. We'd like to have the psychiatrist assess her when she's alert."

Barbara and Tom both nodded, absorbing his words with a sense of calm. "We'll do that," Barbara promised. Dr. Patel gave them both a reassuring nod before the team finished up their work and filed out of the room.

Father Thomas stood, gathering his belongings as Barbara and Tom thanked him for his overnight stay and support. He waved off their gratitude with a gentle smile. "I'm happy to help, truly. It's a blessing to be here for you all."

Barbara's face brightened, and she placed a gentle hand on his arm. "Thank you, Father Thomas. Your presence has been a great comfort. I'll try to stay here as much as I can, but it's hard with the kids and the house to keep up with."

Father Thomas nodded knowingly, his eyes warm with understanding. "Of course, Barbara. I'll keep you all in my prayers."

With one last glance at Linda, he turned and quietly made his way toward the door, his footsteps soft against the sterile hospital floor. Barbara watched him go, a deep gratitude settling in her chest. His presence had been a steady comfort through these long, uncertain days.

She exhaled slowly and turned to Tom, the exhaustion of the past few days still weighing on her, but now, there was something else—a small flicker of hope.

"She looks better, don't you think?" Barbara asked, her voice lighter than it had been in days.

Tom studied Linda for a moment, noting the slight return of color to her cheeks, the way her breathing seemed steadier, calmer. He nodded. "Yeah… she's definitely looking less pale. That's a good sign."

For the first time in what felt like forever, Barbara allowed herself a small smile. It wasn't much, but it was something—a glimmer of reassurance in the long road ahead.

With a gentle smile, she leaned closer and motioned to the nurse nearby. "Could you please page Dr. Patel? Linda's awake."

The nurse gave a quick nod and left the room, returning moments later with Dr. Patel, who entered swiftly. He offered Barbara and Tom a nod as he assessed Linda, noting her steady gaze and calm breathing.

After a brief observation, Dr. Patel stepped away and picked up his phone. "I'll call the psychiatrist," he informed Barbara and Tom. "She's already briefed on Linda's case and should be here shortly."

Not long after, a woman in a neat blouse and kind expression entered the room. She introduced herself as Dr.

Emily Grace, the psychiatrist. She approached Linda gently, her demeanor calm and soothing.

"Hello, Linda," she said softly, her voice filled with empathy. "I'm Dr. Grace. I'm just here to check in with you and see how you're feeling."

Linda's gaze was uncertain, flickering between Barbara, Tom, and Dr. Grace. Her face held a hint of confusion, a trace of disorientation lingering in her expression. Dr. Grace observed her carefully, her trained eyes picking up on Linda's subtle cues.

After a few moments of conversation and assessment, Dr. Grace stepped back. She turned to Barbara and Tom with a soft smile.

"It appears Linda is experiencing a condition known as delirium," she explained. "This is common in patients who have been sedated and in critical care. The amnesia and confusion are temporary, and they often improve with time, especially when the patient is surrounded by familiar faces and routines."

Barbara's face softened with relief as she took in Dr. Grace's words. "So… she'll remember us eventually?"

Dr. Grace nodded reassuringly. "Yes. The brain needs time to heal and adjust. Delirium can be unsettling, but with consistent care and support, Linda's memory and clarity should return."

Tom, who had been quietly absorbing the information, let out a sigh of relief. "Thank you, Doctor. This helps a lot."

Dr. Grace spent a few more minutes explaining what Barbara and Tom could do to support Linda's recovery, emphasizing the importance of familiar voices, gentle interactions, and patience. Barbara listened intently, holding on to each word as though it were a lifeline.

As Dr. Grace and Dr. Patel prepared to leave, Dr. Grace offered one last reassuring smile, her presence a steadying force. Barbara and Tom exchanged glances, feeling a renewed sense of hope and direction settle over them.

Tom let out a small chuckle, shaking his head. "Seems they all take courses on smiling nicely in medical school. Every single one of them is so damn pleasant."

Barbara bit back a laugh, not wanting to startle Linda. Instead, she squeezed Tom's hand lightly. "That's how it should be," she murmured, her voice carrying a softness that hadn't been there in days.

They settled back into their seats, the weight of uncertainty easing, if only a little. Barbara reached for her daughter's hand, brushing her thumb gently over Linda's fingers.

For the first time in what felt like forever, she allowed herself to believe.

Linda would find her way back to them.

Chapter Twenty-One:
JJ Verifies Ron and Frank's Alibis

J J got up and headed for the office. Once inside he greeted everyone and headed toward his office. Once inside he sat and looked up at the Gardner Police Department. He dialed the number.

"Gardner Police Department where can I transfer your call?"

"Hello, this is James Jason of the Rockland Police Department. I'd like to speak to someone about an alleged car accident a week to ten days ago."

"Transferring you now."

There was ringing and then someone answered, "Knox."

"Hello, this is James Jason from the Rockland Police Department. I know you're probably busier than we are, but I'm investigating a hit-and-run accident in Warren. I've got a guy here with a banged-up car who says he was towing a U-Haul behind his vehicle about a week to ten days ago and was hit by someone who ran a red light. Is there any way you could verify that? His name is Ron Whitlow."

"Sure, I can look it up, but it'll take a while. Can I call you back?"

"Yes, and if I don't answer, it's okay to leave a message." JJ gave him his office number.

Next, he took out his pad to start calling Frank's alibis. The first number had no answer, of course, so he left a message.

The next number a man answered.

"Hello, this is James Jason of the Rockland Police Department. Is this Jim?"

"Yes, what's this about?"

"Did you take your bike to the demolition derby last Tuesday?"

"Yes, why?"

"Could you tell me who was with you?"

He rattled off some of the names on the list including Frank.

"Thanks, you've been very helpful."

They both hung up.

He called the next name on the list and a man answered.

"Hello, this is James Jason of the Rockland Police Department. Is this Mark?"

"Yes."

"Did you take your bike to the demolition derby last Tuesday?"

"Yes, why?"

"Who went with you?"

"Why?"

"I am investigating an accident."

"Well, that's the whole point of a demolition derby."

"I realize that. Could you tell me who went with you?"

Mark recited some of the names on the list including Frank.

"Thanks, you've been helpful."

JJ hung up. He wondered how many more he should contact. If Frank had gotten to one of them; he had gotten to all of them. For now, he decided Frank had an alibi.

While he was thinking his phone rang.

"Detective James," he answered.

It was Knox from Gardner.

"I looked up the accident you inquired about and Frank Whitlow was hit by someone who ran a redlight last week. Do you need any details?"

"No, but thanks so much for your time. You've been a big help."

"Over and out," said Knox.

They hung up.

I'm running out of suspects thought JJ unless one of the guys at the bar including Tom had hit Linda.

Chapter Twenty-Two:
The Psychiatrist

Afternoons at the medical center carried a kind of quiet that felt almost like an isolation center. It was different from the bustling mornings filled with ward rounds, the hurried footsteps of nurses, and the constant chatter among doctors. As the sun reached its zenith, casting a golden glow through the windows, the corridors seemed to relax, with silence taking over from the busy morning. It is during this peaceful time that Dr. Grace preferred to visit her patients, including Linda. She loves working without the interruptions of other medical staff bustling in and out. By working around this time, she could devote her full attention to her patient, engaging in the slow and delicate work of guiding them back to their former self. Today was one of those afternoons.

Linda had been moved out of the ICU a few days ago, transitioning to a private room in the main ward—a significant step forward in her recovery. The ICU had been a space of urgency, where every beep and alarm signaled potential catastrophe. Now, the ward was quieter, more serene, a place where healing could take its natural course. Most importantly, Linda was stable, no longer at immediate risk of needing urgent intervention.

Over the past few days, she had made steady improvements. Dr. Grace had been diligent in her behavioral therapy sessions, carefully coaxing fragments of Linda's memory back to the surface. At her suggestion, the room had been transformed into a more familiar and comforting space: photographs of Linda's family adorned the walls, and small mementos from happier times were placed within her view. A framed picture of Linda, Tom, and Barbara on a beach vacation sat on the bedside table, next to a small potted plant. These familiar faces and objects were meant to ground her, to create a bridge between the reality she once knew and the one she was slowly rediscovering.

Father Thomas had spent another night at the hospital, allowing Barbara a few precious hours at home. The nights had been long, but they were made bearable by the unwavering support of friends and family. Barbara arrived early in the morning to relieve him; her eyes were tired, but her spirits lifted. Seeing Linda was a balm to her weary soul. Tom had come later in the morning after a quick stop at his garage. He had hoped to catch up on work, but his thoughts were never far from the medical center.

Now, Barbara sat in the chair beside Linda's bed, her eyes softening as she watched her daughter. Linda was fiddling with a remote control, turning it over in her hands with the curiosity of a child. It was a small, almost insignificant moment, but to Barbara, it felt like a miracle. After weeks of uncertainty and fear, Linda was beginning to return, piece by piece, to the woman she had always been. The joy in Barbara's heart was almost overwhelming.

"Linda, are you figuring out how that thing works?" Barbara asked with a light-hearted smile, trying to keep the atmosphere relaxed.

Linda looked up; her eyes briefly filled with surprise before she responded. "Of course I do, Mom," she replied, her voice soft, almost fragile. "I'm not that bad," she added, with a little smile.

"Absolutely darling, you're in great shape. I just thought…you know, with the way you were fiddling it"

"Don't mind your mom. She's just being her typical self" Tom said, sinking into the armchair beside Barbara.

Linda placed the remote down, her gaze shifting to the photos on the wall as if they might unlock something in her mind.

"Who's that over there?" Linda asked, picking at a picture of her and another lady.

"Oh, that's Nancy. She was here earlier this morning, but you were still asleep."

"Is she my sister?" Linda asked, a bit confused.

"No, no. Far from it. She's your friend." Barbara didn't want to bother her with the details of her relationship with Nancy. It's too early for all that drama.

"Actually, her dog, Cody, found you and kept barking until Linda went to get him; she found you and called an ambulance. So, in a way, the dog and Nancy saved your life."

'Tom looked from Barbara to Linda, then shrugged.

Barbara took a deep breath, her eyes flicking to the wall clock. The minute hand inched closer to 2 PM. Dr. Grace was always punctual, arriving like clockwork for her afternoon sessions. Barbara had come to depend on these visits, knowing they were helping Linda find her way out of the fog.

A few moments later, the door to the room opened, and Dr. Grace stepped in. Dressed in her usual neat attire, she carried an air of calm professionalism. There was a warmth in her eyes that had a way of putting both patients and their loved ones at ease. She greeted Barbara and Tom with a reassuring smile, her gaze briefly assessing Linda's condition.

"Good afternoon, Mr. and Mrs. Berry. How are things today?" she asked.

Tom gave his usual nod, while Barbara returned the smile, though the exhaustion on her face was unmistakable. "We're doing better, I think. Linda's been playing with things while in bed. It's... it's good to see her like this."

Dr. Grace nodded, her expression softening as she turned to Linda. "That's wonderful progress."

She stepped toward the bed with a practiced gentleness, as if entering a delicate ecosystem, she was careful not to disturb.

As Dr. Grace made her way to Linda's bedside, Barbara hesitated before speaking. "Doctor, I've been reading a bit about therapies in situations like this, and I was wondering - would Cognitive Behavioral Therapy help Linda improve faster? I've read that it can be effective in treating memory issues and many other psychological conditions."

Dr. Grace paused thoughtfully, considering Barbara's question. "CBT can be very effective in certain contexts," she began, "but it requires the patient to engage in structured, constructive conversations, focusing on cognitive patterns and behaviors. In cases like Linda's, where acute amnesia is present, it's often too soon for that approach. At this time, we're focusing on helping her re-establish a sense of familiarity and safety. Once she's further along, we can explore therapies like CBT."

Barbara nodded slowly, absorbing the information. "Thank you, Dr. Grace. I just... I want to make sure we're doing everything we can."

"And you both are," Dr. Grace reassured her. "You're doing wonderfully, Mrs. Berry. The progress Linda has made so far is due, in no small part, to the love and support she's getting from you and Mr. Berry."

"And to the medical team too. You've all been amazing at your job" Tom said.

Dr. Grace turned her attention back to Linda, who was watching the conversation unfold with some curiosity. There was confusion in her eyes too. The psychiatrist leaned in closer, her voice soft. "Linda, how are you feeling today? Do you remember where you are?"

Linda blinked, her eyes scanning the room before she nodded. "I'm... in the hospital, right?"

"That's right," Dr. Grace said with an encouraging smile. "You're doing great, Linda. I know you may feel confused, but you're making wonderful progress. Do you remember me?"

"Yes, you're Dr. Emily Grace."

"That's a brilliant answer."

After asking a few more questions to assess Linda's awareness and memory, Dr. Grace shifted the conversation gently. "I've noticed that your delirium has resolved," she said reassuringly. "Now, our focus is on helping your memory return."

She paused for a moment before continuing. "I'm going to prescribe a low dose of Risperidone to help stabilize your mood. And now that you're out of the ICU, we can allow more visitors. Seeing familiar faces should help trigger more memories."

Linda nodded, but her brow furrowed as if she were struggling to put a puzzle together. "Why... why can't I remember the accident? Or how I got here?"

Dr. Grace's expression softened. "Sometimes, after a trauma like the one you've experienced, the brain tries to protect itself by blocking out those memories. It's like a survival mechanism. But with time, those memories might start to come back."

Dr. Grace finished her session, offering a few more reassurances before she excused herself to see her other patients. Barbara watched her go, feeling satisfied with her intervention but with loads of questions in her mind. She was grateful for the steady presence of Dr. Grace, but each answer seemed to raise new questions.

As soon as Dr. Grace left, Linda turned to her mother, her eyes now sharper and more focused than they had been in days. "Mom, how did the accident happen? Was anyone else hurt?"

Barbara's heart clenched, but she kept her voice steady. "Linda, sweetheart, you've been through so much. Let's not worry about that right now. Focus on getting better."

Linda's face scrunched up in frustration. "But I need to know... Did they catch the driver who hit me?"

Barbara hesitated, her eyes shifting briefly to Tom, who was standing by the window. Sweat had started to bead on Tom's forehead, and he quickly wiped it away with the back of his hand. His face had gone slightly pale, and his hands trembled slightly as he gripped the windowsill.

"Linda," Tom said, his voice rough, "your mom's right. You should focus on getting better. We can talk about all that later, okay?"

Linda's eyes narrowed, catching the unease in Tom's voice, but she was too tired to press further. She leaned back into her pillows, her eyes closing as she tried to recall what had happened that night. It was like reaching into a dark, bottomless pit - no matter how hard she tried, she couldn't grasp hold of anything solid. She opened her eyes and looked at the clock. It was almost 6 PM.

Tom, desperate to escape the tension in the room, mumbled something about needing a drink of water and quickly left. Barbara watched him go, her brow furrowed with concern. She knew Tom was struggling, but she didn't have the energy to confront him about it—not now, when Linda needed them so much. Starting an argument wouldn't help her condition in any way.

As Linda lay back, she let her thoughts drift, trying to piece together the fragments of her shattered memories.

She could recall flashes—her mother's laughter, the smell of Tom's cologne, the feeling of sunshine on her skin. But the accident itself remained a dark void. It was like a missing piece in the jigsaw puzzle of her mind—one that left the entire picture incomplete.

She sighed, closing her eyes. She knew she had a long way to go, but at least she was alive. At least she had her family by her side. For now, that would have to be enough. She would have to patiently wait for the remaining memories to return from their voyage.

. .
.

Linda came back awake, her eyelids fluttering open to the dim glow of the bedside lamp. The room was covered in the gentle silence of the evening. For a moment, she was disoriented, the haze of sleep still lingering. As her vision cleared, she saw Tom seated in the chair by her bed, his head tilted slightly downward, lost in thought.

She blinked, adjusting to the dim light. Her gaze drifted toward the clock on the wall. The hands pointed to 8:35 PM. It had been late afternoon when she last remembered speaking with Dr. Grace. "Dad?" she called softly, her voice still laced with fatigue.

Tom looked up, his face immediately brightening. "Hey, you're awake," he said, leaning forward. There was relief in his eyes.

"Where's Mom?" Linda asked, glancing around as if expecting Barbara to be seated in the corner of the room, where she usually was.

Tom paused for a moment, then offered a gentle smile. "She went home, Linda. She needed to check on the house and your children," he explained.

"My... children?" Linda frowned the words sounding foreign in her ears. The confusion was like a fog closing in around her thoughts. "I have... children?"

Tom's heart clenched at the look of distress that flashed across her face. He thought maybe he should have waited a bit before telling her. "Well, the deed is done." he thought to himself as he reached for her hand, squeezing it reassuringly. "Yes, you do. Beautiful kids who miss you a lot," he said softly. "They can't wait to see you, and I promise, once they visit, everything will start coming back to you. Seeing them might just jog your memory."

Linda looked down at their joined hands, her eyes brimming with tears. The thought that she had children she couldn't remember - children who were waiting for her and needed her felt like another blow to an already fractured mind. "I wish I could remember them," she whispered, her voice trembling. "I feel like I've lost so much of myself."

Tom's grip tightened just a little, trying to convey the strength he wished he could give her. "You haven't lost anything, Linda. It's all still there," he reassured her, though he could hear the uncertainty in his own voice. "We're all here for you, every step of the way. And we'll get through this together."

Linda nodded, though a deep sadness lingered in her eyes. She tried to draw comfort from Tom's words, but the emptiness in her mind left her feeling hollow. She turned her face away from him, staring at the ceiling, letting herself drift back into the darkness that sleep offered.

As her eyes closed, she silently wished that this torturous phase would soon end. She hoped she would wake up one day with everything restored and all the memories that made her Linda Berry finally return.

Chapter Twenty-Three:
JJ Interviews Linda

J had driven around looking at the cars of the men from the Roadhouse. None of them looked damaged or recently repaired except Tom's. Finally, he headed to the medical center. The doctors had agreed to a five-minute interview with Linda.

He crossed the parking lot knowing he could be intimidating and tried to think of a few questions that might help but not trigger her.

Once inside, he headed for the ICU. He pushed the red button and eventually, a nurse let him in.

"I'm here to see Linda Williams," he said

"Oh, she moved to another room because of her improvement. Just continue down this corridor and take your first right. She is on that unit now room 205".

JJ followed her instructions and found room 205. Linda was in bed, awake, holding her mother's hand. JJ knocked softly and entered the room.

"Nice to see you, Detective James," Barbara said. "Why don't you take my chair?"

She stood up and moved to another chair. JJ sat down next to Linda.

"Do you remember me?" he asked.

"Your face is familiar, but I can't remember your name," she responded.

"I am a detective, but you can call me JJ."

"Okay."

"I hear you were in a terrible accident."

"Yes, but I don't remember anything until a few days ago when I woke up and even then, I was confused."

"What I am assuming is that you went for a walk after dark and were hit by a car."

"That's what they tell me."

"You don't remember hearing a car coming, getting hit or seeing the car at all?"

"No, not yet."

"Well, if anything comes to mind, tell your mother and she will call me. I'm glad to see you're on the mend."

JJ stood up, said goodbye to Barbara and left.

. .
.

He headed back to the ICU and pushed the red button again. This time he didn't have to wait as long. A nurse opened the door and said, "Can I help you?"

"Could you take me to Nancy King's office?"

She led the way.

Nancy was sitting at her desk reading some papers. She looked up.

"Oh, what a nice surprise. What brings you here?"

"I wanted to find out what time Bill's game is tomorrow night."

"It's at 7 pm in Augusta."

"Let's leave about 5 and stop for a bite to eat."

"The other two kids will be coming."

"They need to eat."

"You're going to feed us all?"

"Sure."

"Then let's leave at 4. I want to stop at the Chevy Dealership."

"Why?"

"You'll see. It's a secret for now."

"Okay, I'll pick you all up at 4."

JJ said goodbye and left.

Chapter Twenty-Four:
Bills Basketball Game

JJ sat in his office all day going over reports and notes. The results of the paint chips he had found near the Roadhouse sign were generic blue and Chevy silver. the suspects he had eliminated making sure they were truly alibied. At this point Tom still seemed the most likely. Drunk as he was, he could have had two accidents.

He organized his reports and notes for future reference, then, at exactly 3:30 p.m., he set off for Nancy's house. When he arrived, the excitement was already in the air—everyone was ready and waiting, not just for the game, but for the promise of dinner out afterward.

They all piled into the car, Nancy sliding into the front seat beside JJ, while Debbie and Bob settled comfortably in the back.

"Seatbelts on, please," JJ reminded them with a smile. They complied without a word, too eager for the evening ahead to argue.

The drive to Augusta was filled with word games and laughter, their cheerful voices mingling with the soft hum of music from the radio. Time passed quickly, and before they knew it, JJ was pulling into the lot of a Chevy dealership.

"So now I get to find out the big secret," he muttered under his breath, casting a curious glance at Nancy.

Nancy turned to the kids, her voice calm but firm. "Stay in the car and be good—no fighting. We've got a little business to take care of with the dealer, but it won't take long. Then we're off to dinner."

With a wink and a smile, she stepped out of the car, leaving the kids buzzing with curiosity in the backseat, their imaginations already running wild.

As they walked to the showroom of the dealership, Nancy said," I need you to be a detective and find out all you can about Father Thomas' car; the repairs, any parts left over etc. Can you do this for me?"

"I really don't see the point but I will humor you one more time."

As they entered the building JJ walked up to a salesman, introduced himself as Detective James from the Rockland Police and showed his badge.

"We would like to talk to the owner," he said.

The salesman led them to one of the back offices and introduced them to the manager. They all shook hands and sat down.

"The owner's not here but Mr. Trumbull can probably answer all your questions," he said and left.

"What can I do for you detective," Mr. Trumbull asked?

"A couple weeks ago a priest, Father Thomas, brought a car here for repairs. It was a blue Chevy SUV. I am interested in the problem with the car and what was fixed," said JJ.

"I'll never forget that one it was the one of the strangest incidents I've dealt with. The right front fender was bent, the right light was smashed and the bumper was in the back of the car. He said he hit a deer. I gave him an estimate to fix it, but he didn't want it fixed. He wanted to trade it in and get a used one just like it in blue. He said something about not wanting to drive a car that had been in an accident."

"We gave him a loaner and found one like his in Massachusetts. It took a day to get the one from Mass up here. When the car arrived, he came up, paid the difference and drove off."

"Where is his original car now" asked JJ?

"We fixed it and sold it in a couple days to some guy in Hallowell who wanted a four-wheel drive with all those hills there."

"Do you have the paperwork so I can get his name, address and phone number?"

"Sure, it's in the file here somewhere."

Mr. Trumbull opened a drawer in the file cabinet and shuffled through all the files and finally said, "here it is."

"Could you make a copy of this for me," asked JJ?

Mr. Trumbull left the office and came back with a copy. "Did we do something wrong or was the priest unhappy with the new/used car? I'm curious what this is all about."

"You did nothing wrong. I am investigating an accident and you have been more than helpful. Thank you for all the information."

They all shook hands again, said goodbye then JJ and Nancy left. When they got back to the car Debbie and Bob were sitting quietly acting on their best behavior.

"We have a lot of choices here. What does everyone want to eat?" JJ asked?

"Let's drive down Water Street and see what looks good," said Nancy.

JJ headed for Water Street, which was a challenge as it was one way. But they went across the bridge crossing the Kennebec River, turned left and started down Water Street looking at all the restaurants.

"Oh," Nancy said, "my friends have raved about State lunch. They have a great variety and there will be something everyone likes."

JJ drove on and finally found a parking place. They all piled out of the car and headed for the restaurant; Debbie skipping all the way with Bob trying to keep up.

. .
.

Once they got through the menu, which was no easy task for Debbie and Bob, who wanted almost everything, they finally made their choices. As they waited for their food, JJ told some lame jokes, earning dramatic groans from the kids.

Despite the eye-rolling, laughter filled the table, and the conversation flowed easily. When their meals arrived, the chatter quieted as everyone dug in, enjoying the meal.

After dinner, the kids immediately asked for dessert. Nancy glanced at her watch. "If it's okay with JJ, you can have dessert—but we'll have to take it to go. We don't want to be late for the game."

Debbie and Bob quickly agreed, each choosing ice cream in a paper cup. JJ paid the bill, and soon, they were heading back to the car, the excitement of the upcoming game buzzing between them.

. .
.

Once they got to the game the parking lot was overflowing.

"You all get out and I will find a place to park and meet you inside," JJ said.

They got out and JJ drove around until he found a spot on a side street. He memorized the street name and headed for the building where the game was being held. When he got inside, Nancy was waiting for him at the door.

"I told the kids to get us seats, it's filling up fast."

They headed to where the kids were sitting and JJ sat between Debbie and Nancy. The cheerleaders were cheering and when they stopped, the bands played. Finally, the players emerged and the game started.

Both teams were pretty even in the first quarter. Then Bill's team fell behind. At halftime, the other team was up 6 points. As they went off to the locker rooms, Bob and Debbie asked for popcorn. JJ got in line and waited. Before halftime ended, he made it to the counter and ordered 3 boxes of popcorn.

He took the popcorn back to their seats amid cheering and bands. He could hardly hear Nancy when she asked why he bought three.

"I thought we could share one," he said.

I'm still full from dinner," she replied.

Then the game started again. Bill's team came out all fired up, scored, stole the ball and scored again. It was on. The two teams went back and forth until the very end. Then one of Bill's teammates was fouled while shooting. They were tied. He had two shots. He missed the first and Debbie finished the popcorn she had been eating out of nervousness. He made the second shot and Bill's team won. Everyone on their side cheered.

Debbie, Bob and Nancy all looked very happy. They went up to congratulate Bill.

JJ said, "I'll go get the car."

"No," said Nancy, "you'll never find us in this traffic."

Okay, but it's quite a walk."

"That's not a problem. We'll have to wait for Bill's bus when we get home and they will probably stop to eat on the way."

"I don't want to wait for Bill's bus," whined Debbie. Why didn't you ask him to get a ride home with a friend?"

"I'll drop you all off and return to wait for the bus," said JJ.

"You don't have to do that," said Nancy.

"The kids are tired and I don't mind,"

As they drove home, the kids did fall asleep and Debbie had to wake them to get them in the house. They were grumpy but did as she asked.

"I guess you were right," she said. "And Cody has been home alone for a long time. Thank you for dinner and for picking up Bill. I hope it wasn't too boring for you."

"I enjoyed it. And I also enjoyed getting to know your children better. We'll have to do it again sometime,"

JJ drove to the school to wait for the bus along with a lot of other parents. It didn't take long for it to arrive. Bill got out and looked for his mother's car so JJ got out and waved at him.

"Why are you picking me up?" he asked.

"Debbie and Bob fell asleep on the way home, so I volunteered to drop everyone off and come back to pick you up," JJ said with a grin. "Great game, by the way. You must be excited."

"I'm just glad I wasn't the one at the foul line for those final shots," Bill replied, chuckling softly.

They drove the rest of the way in companionable silence, the quiet hum of the road filling the space between them.

When they pulled into the driveway, JJ reached over to open the back door and grabbed his gym bag.

"Say goodnight to your mother for me," he said. "Tell her I'd come in, but I've got a long day ahead tomorrow."

Bill gave a nod and headed into the house without another word.

JJ drove home, the night settling around him. Once there, he washed up, climbed into bed, and drifted into sleep—his thoughts full of Nancy.

Chapter Twenty-Five:
Linda Prepares for Rehab

I t had been a few days since Linda had been on the ward, and life on the regular ward felt like a breath of fresh air. The sterile, isolating walls of the intensive care unit were now replaced by a slightly more welcoming room, with sunlight streaming through the window. There were still beeping machines and the occasional scent of antiseptic, but now there was also laughter, warmth, and the presence of loved ones filling the room.

Linda's journey had turned a corner, shifting from uncertainty to hope. The steady stream of visitors—her children, extended family, and close friends—had become a lifeline, anchoring her to the life she was slowly reclaiming. Each familiar face, each shared story, wove together the frayed edges of her memory, drawing her closer to the person she used to be.

With every passing day, more fragments returned—her daughter's infectious giggle echoing in her mind, the way her son's eyes sparkled with excitement when he spoke about his latest school project, the warmth of her mother's embrace. The once-gaping void that had consumed her after waking in the hospital was no longer as daunting. It was filling, piece by piece, with love, familiarity, and a sense of belonging.

Dr. Grace, who had been her guiding light through the haze of confusion, no longer needed to visit daily. The intense therapy sessions of the first few days had eased into check-ins every three days—a testament to Linda's remarkable progress.

Her hospital room, once a sterile space of monitors and machines, had transformed into a haven of warmth and comfort. Photographs of cherished moments lined the walls, colorful drawings from her children brightened the bedside table, and a soft, well-worn blanket from home now covered her legs. These small tokens, carefully arranged under Dr. Grace's guidance, served as gentle reminders of the life waiting for her beyond the hospital walls.

Piece by piece, Linda was stitching herself back together.

This morning, Linda lay propped up on her pillows with the sun casting a glow on her face. She felt different as if she were stepping out of a long, dark tunnel and finally seeing the light. Barbara had stayed overnight to keep her company. Father Thomas was tied up with church activities and so couldn't stay the night as he usually did. Tom had been unable to stay due to a mild fever, but he was feeling better now and had come back to the hospital early in the morning.

Barbara stood by the window, looking out at the bustling courtyard below, while Tom sat in a chair beside Linda's bed, holding her hand. He looked much better after taking his medication, though there was still a slight pallor to his skin.

"I'm so glad to see you looking better, Dad," Linda said.

"I couldn't stay away, you know that. But I'm doing fine now. Just needed a little rest," he replied. Then, turning to Barbara, he added, "You should go home and rest now. You've been here all night."

Barbara shook her head. "I'll go after the morning rounds. I want to hear what Dr. Patel has to say about the scan," she insisted, her voice firm.

Linda tried to persuade her. "Mom, you really don't have to stay. I promise I'll update you on everything the doctors say."

Barbara simply waved her off. "I'm not going anywhere until I hear it myself," she said, her eyes filled with that stubborn resolve Linda knew so well. Finally, both Linda and Tom gave up trying to convince her otherwise.

The minutes ticked by slowly as they waited for the doctors to arrive. Linda's mind wandered to the events of the past few days. She marveled at how much progress she had made yet there were still blank spots in her memory that felt like missing pages in a book she was eager to read. She was brought out of her thoughts by the sound of footsteps and the familiar creak of the door.

Dr. Patel walked in with Dr. Roberts and nurse Abigail. They were followed by a young intern, who carried a stack of charts. Linda straightened up a bit, her heart fluttering with anticipation. This was the moment they had all been waiting for - the results of the brain CT scan.

Dr. Patel greeted everyone warmly, his presence carrying the steady reassurance they had come to rely on. As always, his expression exuded calm confidence.

"Good morning," he said, his voice even and composed. "I've reviewed the CT scan we did yesterday."

With practiced ease, he walked over to the lightbox on the wall, placing the scan film carefully onto it. The bright glow illuminated the intricate details of Linda's brain, casting subtle shadows that only the trained eyes of a neurosurgeon could truly interpret.

"From what I can see," Dr. Patel began, gesturing toward a specific section on the film, "the edema has significantly reduced, and the intracerebral hematoma has shrunk. That's fantastic progress."

He turned toward Barbara and Tom, his expression softening into a genuine smile, the corners of his eyes crinkling slightly. "She's healed remarkably well compared to the last scan we did."

Linda couldn't help but smile, a sense of triumph bubbling within her. She was healing. She was truly on the mend.

Dr. Roberts was already at the bedside to examine Linda's leg. "Let's see how this is doing," he said as he gently prodded the area around her surgical wound. "Looks good," he announced. "The wound has healed very well, and it's time to get you out of bed."

Linda's eyes widened. "Really? I can get out of bed now?"

Dr. Roberts nodded, his face breaking into a grin. "Yes, but first, we'll need to fit you with a fiberglass cast to stabilize your leg. It'll be a little while before you can bear weight on it, so you'll start with a wheelchair. Then, once you've built up some strength, we'll move on to crutches."

He looked at Linda with a twinkle in his eye. "The cast comes in different colors, you know. Which one would you like?"

Linda's face lit up with excitement. "Pink! I've always loved pink."

Tom chuckled, his eyes softening as he looked at his daughter. "That's true. She's always had a thing for pink," he said, sharing a knowing wink with Dr. Roberts.

The doctors finished their examinations and updated the charts. Before leaving, Dr. Patel reminded them that the next steps would involve starting Linda on some gentle physical therapy. "We'll work slowly," he assured them. "The goal is to rebuild her strength little by little."

As the doctors and nurse exited the room, Barbara watched them go, a look of profound relief washing over her face. "I'm so happy, Linda. You're finally getting better," she said, leaning over to kiss her daughter's forehead.

Tom, ever the practical one, gently reminded her, "You promised to go home after the ward round, remember?"

Linda nodded in agreement. "He's right, Mom. You've been here since yesterday. Go home and rest, please."

Barbara finally relented, her shoulders slumping in exhaustion. "Alright, alright," she said, gathering her things. "But only because you both insist." With one last kiss on Linda's forehead, she made her way out of the room.

After Barbara left, the room settled into a soft stillness, the steady rhythm of the monitors filling the space. Tom exhaled, shifting his chair closer to Linda's bedside. Without hesitation, he took her hand in his, his thumb brushing lightly over her fingers.

"You're doing so well, Linda," he said, his voice low but full of warmth.

Linda met his gaze, her eyes shimmering with gratitude. "I'm just glad to be here… to be alive." She paused, her lips curving into a small, thoughtful smile. "It's been such a long road, but I'm finally seeing the light at the end of the tunnel."

Tom squeezed her hand gently, his own emotions flickering just beneath the surface. "We're getting through this together," he assured her. "One step at a time."

For a moment, neither of them spoke. They didn't need to. The unspoken understanding between them—the quiet strength, the unwavering support—was enough.

For a while, they simply sat there, talking about little things - the weather, the garage, and Tom's plans for when Linda was finally discharged from the hospital. It was the kind of conversation that felt normal, almost boring, and that in itself was a gift.

In that moment, surrounded by love and light, Linda allowed herself to believe that everything would be alright. She was healing, slowly but surely. And with her family by her side, she knew she would find her way back to herself again.

Chapter Twenty-Six:
JJ Finds Something Under Father Thomas's Car

JJ awoke, put the coffee on and took a shower while it was brewing. He got dressed, went downstairs and had a cup black. He was thinking about Nancy and her good instincts. Either that or he was about to run a fool's errand. It did seem suspicious though that Father Tomas would get rid of his car.

He toasted a bagel to go with his second cup of coffee, the rich aroma filling the quiet morning air. As he ate, he spread the papers from the Chevy Dealership across the table, scanning them with a practiced eye. The details were all there, but a direct conversation would be more efficient— if he could avoid ruffling any feathers. It was still a little early to make calls without risking irritation, and the last thing he needed was a reluctant witness. A warrant would only slow things down.

Instead, he reached for his phone and dialed the police station. "Just checking in," he told the Desk Sergeant. "I'll be out following up on a lead, but call if anything urgent comes up." The sergeant assured him the message would be passed along.

Still biding his time, he gathered up a pile of laundry and started a load, letting the hum of the washing machine fill the silence. He'd make his call soon—but for now, a little patience might go a long way.

Finally, he couldn't stand it any longer so he picked up the phone and dialed. A woman answered.

He said," Good morning this is Detective James Jason of the Rockland police. I'm looking for Brad Huff."

"He's not here right now. He went for a walk."

"Do you know when he will be back?"

"Not exactly. It depends on how many people he runs into on his walk and how long they talk. What is this about anyway?"

"I am working on a case that involves the blue Chevy SUV he bought recently. It has nothing to do with you or him. It has to do with the previous owner."

"Are there drugs stashed in that car or something else illegal?"

"No, nothing like that, I would just like to examine the car with your permission, of course,"

"I guess you're welcome to come take a look if you like, but while you're on your way, I am going to call the Rockland Police to see if you are on the up and up. And bring your badge and identification with you. There are so many people scamming and taking advantage of older retired people these days I don't trust anyone. Brad should be home by the time you get here,"

"You are absolutely right Mrs. Huff to be safety conscious and I will have my badge and identification with me. I would also be comfortable waiting until your husband gets home."

"Thank you. I will see you in a while, officer. Goodbye."

Gosh he thought as he grabbed his jacket to leave. What has this world come to? She was a sharp woman, but it saddened him to think that people had to be so hypervigilant these days. He walked out, got in his car making sure he had his badge and ID.

As he drove to Hallowell, he thought it was lucky he had been too lazy to bring the Luminol back to the station. That was one stop he wouldn't have to make. Traffic on Route 17 was thinning out as people got to their jobs. The drive was nice and he remembered a shortcut through Gardiner that would save him time. He could also stop at Boley's and get a couple of their delicious donuts if they weren't sold out.

He arrived at the Huffs in about half an hour. Mr. Huff was right about the hills. They lived on a side street about halfway up one of them. That hill was long and steep. As he pulled up to their house, he saw the blue Chevy in the driveway.

He got out of his car with his badge and ID in his hand and knocked on the door. A gray-haired man who looked to be in his late sixties or seventy opened the door.

"Detective Jason", he said, holding out his hand to shake. My wife told me you were coming so I took the car out of the garage to make it easier for you to examine."

"Thank you so much Mr. Huff. You can call me JJ, that's my nickname."

"Well in that case JJ, you can call me Brad. Now what exactly do you need to look at on my car and why? Is it unsafe to drive?"

"No, no, it's nothing like that. We had a hit and run accident before you bought the car and we're checking lots of cars."

"The salesman told me it belonged to a priest before I bought it. Seems unlikely a priest would be in a hit and run."

"Yes, it does, but we have a job to do and we have to consider anyone a suspect regardless of their job status."

"Well, have at it. Is there anything I can do to help."

"Just don't touch anything until I am done and say it's okay."

JJ grabbed his kit and the bottle of luminol before heading over to inspect the car. At first glance, it was clear that the fender, right headlight, and bumper had been replaced recently—too recently to ignore. He crouched down, peering underneath, scanning for anything out of place. Nothing stood out.

Reaching for the luminol, he sprayed a light mist across the surface, then switched on his flashlight. *Bingo.* A faint glow spread beneath the beam, confirming the presence of blood or another reactant. His instincts had been right.

Without hesitation, JJ retrieved a roll of evidence tape and a knife from his kit. He carefully pressed the tape onto the stained areas, running a smooth object over each piece to ensure proper adhesion. Slipping on gloves, he peeled the tape away and sealed it inside labeled evidence bags.

Next, he took out a small paper bag, methodically scraping residue from the affected areas, ensuring the fine particles fell inside. Once finished, he sealed the paper bag inside another evidence bag, marking it accordingly. Satisfied with the collection process, he took a step back, surveying the car. This was a lead worth following up on.

"I'm all done," he told Brad. "But it would be helpful if you didn't use your car for a couple of days. Do you have another vehicle?"

"Yes, my wife has a car."

"Rather than impound your car I'm going to ask you not to drive it for 72 hours. Could I trust you to do that? Actually, would you mind giving me all the keys for the car?"

"Of course. Was that blood you found?"

"Most likely but it could be racoon blood, squirrel blood, deer blood. I have no way of telling if it's human blood. As soon as it's tested, I'll see that you get your keys back from the State Police.""

"Oh, and please tell your wife this is not a scam to steal your car."

Brad laughed. "She's had some friends who were foolishly scammed and she'll be damned she's not going to be like them.

Brad got all the car keys and gave them to JJ. He took them and placed them in a bag and labeled them with Brad's name and address. He put his kit away and put his samples in the car.

"Thanks again, Brad, I'm sorry for the inconvenience but you'll have your keys back soon."

JJ got in his car and headed for the State Police in Augusta. He found the building and entered. He explained to the man on desk duty that he had samples to be tested ASAP. Then he asked to speak with whoever was in charge today.

Soon a State Policeman came to the desk.

"I'm Lieutenant Gillespie", he said.

"Hi, I'm Detective James from Rockland. I dropped off some samples to be tested. We have an unsolved hit-and-run and one of the cars involved may have been bought by Brad Huff in Hallowell. He is not a suspect. I didn't want to go to the trouble of impounding his car and he promised not to drive it, but I have all his keys here. Can I get your card and call you when they can be returned?"

The Lieutenant handed him his card. JJ handed him the keys.

"Would you please be responsible to see that the keys are returned when I call you. His address and phone are on the bag?"

"Impounding his car would be proper procedure, but it is a pain and I think this will work. I will make sure he gets his keys back as soon as you call."

"Thanks so much," said JJ and he left.

The drive home was uneventful. He went to the police station and returned the luminol. He sat in his office and looked over all his notes. This blood sample was his last prospect and he hoped it wouldn't be Father Thomas.

Chapter Twenty-Seven:
Rehab Completed:
Linda Discharged Home

The cast on Linda's leg had finally been set, a necessary but uncomfortable reminder of how far she still had to go. Yet, the heaviness in her heart was now tinged with hope. The doctors' morning rounds had been filled with optimism, particularly Dr. Roberts, who had brought good news during his visit the previous evening. He had told Linda and her mother, Barbara, that she would soon be discharged from the ward and transferred to the Rehabilitation Center. Although a physiotherapist has been seeing her on the ward, she needed more intense therapy. The goal was to help her leg regain its strength and mobility. It was the first real milestone in Linda's journey back to her old life, and the news had brought tears of relief to both mother and daughter.

Now, they found themselves sitting side by side in the waiting room of the physiotherapy department. The sound of soft music played from a distant speaker. Linda glanced around at the motivational posters on the walls - images of people climbing mountains, running marathons, living the kind of active life that felt like a distant dream to her now. She sighed softly, turning her gaze to Barbara, who sat with her hands folded in her lap. Barbara was offering a reassuring smile.

"You'll get there, Linda," Barbara said gently, sensing the worry behind her daughter's quiet eyes. "Just look at how far you've already come. Not that long ago, you were in the ICU—barely conscious. And now, here you are... up, talking, laughing. You're getting stronger every single day."

Linda offered a faint smile, though her eyes shimmered with uncertainty. "I know, Mom. I just... I never imagined it would take this long. Sometimes it feels like I'll never be the same again."

Barbara reached over, resting a comforting hand on her daughter's shoulder. "You will, sweetheart. It just takes time. And we'll be right here with you, every step of the way."

A few moments later, the receptionist called Linda's name, signaling that the physiotherapist was ready to see them. Barbara helped Linda into the wheelchair, and they made their way into the office. The physiotherapist, a tall man with kind eyes named Mr. Daniels, stood up to greet them.

"Good morning, Linda and Barbara. It's a pleasure to meet you both," he said, shaking their hands warmly. "I've gone through your file, Linda, and it's clear you've made tremendous progress since your accident. Let's take a look at where we are today."

Mr. Daniels then conducted a thorough examination of Linda's leg, gently assessing the range of motion and the level of pain she experienced. He nodded thoughtfully as he worked, occasionally making notes in her chart.

"Alright, here's where we stand," he said, stepping back and folding his arms across his chest. "Linda, your leg has healed nicely, but the muscles have weakened significantly due to prolonged immobilization. We're going to focus on strengthening your uninjured leg first to support the fractured one. The goal is to gradually build up your strength so that you can transition from using a wheelchair to using parallel bars, and eventually, crutches."

Barbara leaned forward; her eyes filled with concern. "So, what's your assessment, Doctor? How long do you think it will take before she can walk again?"

"It's hard to put an exact timeline on it, but given Linda's current progress, I'm optimistic. Typically, patients in your condition can take several weeks or even months to regain their full strength. However, I've seen cases where the combination of determination and a strong support system can accelerate recovery. Linda, you have both of those factors in your favor."

He paused, then continued, "To start, we're going to admit you for inpatient care here at the Rehabilitation Center. You'll need intensive, daily physiotherapy and close medical monitoring to ensure there are no complications. We'll be working together every day, Linda, focusing on exercises that will gradually build up your strength."

Linda nodded, trying to absorb all the information. "I understand," she said softly. "I just want to get back on my feet as soon as possible."

"That's the spirit," Mr. Daniels replied with a grin. "We'll start with exercises for your good leg and upper body to prepare you for when you can put weight on your fractured leg. Once you're stable enough, we'll have you practicing with the parallel bars to get you used to bearing weight again. It will be challenging, but I have no doubt that you're up for it."

Barbara and Linda asked a few more questions about the therapy plan, and Mr. Daniels patiently answered each one. Once they were satisfied, he scheduled Linda to begin her rehabilitation program that very afternoon. It felt like the start of a new chapter, and both women left his office feeling cautiously optimistic.

. .
.

The first few days of rehabilitation were nothing short of grueling. What seemed like simple exercises on paper became battles against her own body's limitations. Every movement—every stretch, every lift—was a reminder of how much strength she had lost. Linda's muscles ached, her body protested, and at times, the frustration threatened to consume her.

But she refused to let it win.

Tom and Barbara were always there, their unwavering support a lifeline. When exhaustion threatened to pull her under, their words lifted her up. *You've come so far, Linda. Keep going. You can do this.*

Mr. Daniels, her physical therapist, was a perfect balance of firm and compassionate. He knew exactly when to push and when to let her breathe. "You're doing great,

Linda. Just one more step," he encouraged, his voice steady, unwavering.

Gritting her teeth, she focused on his words, pushing through the burn in her legs. One more lift. One more step. One more victory on the long road ahead.

Gradually, Linda began to see progress. Her muscles felt stronger, and she was able to sit up for longer periods without feeling dizzy or fatigued. After a week of intensive therapy, she reached a significant milestone: she was ready to try using the parallel bars.

"The physiotherapy she had on the ward before coming here has really helped accelerate her recovery. She can be allowed home in less than two weeks if she continues to progress at this rate." Mr. Daniels had said to his assistant during one of the sessions.

With the help of Mr. Daniels and a physical therapy assistant, Linda stood between the bars, her hands gripping them tightly for support. She took a tentative step forward, her legs trembling from the effort. Sweat beaded on her forehead, and for a moment, she thought she would collapse. But with a deep breath and encouragement from Barbara and Mr. Daniels, she managed to take another step, and then another.

"You're doing it, Linda!" Barbara cheered, her eyes glistening with pride. "You're walking!"

Though it was only a few shaky steps, it felt like a monumental achievement to Linda. The sensation of her feet touching the ground, of bearing her own weight after so long, brought tears to her eyes

After that day, the progress seemed to come in leaps and bounds. Linda grew stronger, and each session brought her closer to walking independently. About seventeen days after she first tried the parallel bars, Mr. Daniels called Linda and Barbara into his office for an update.

Dr. Patel was sitting behind Mr. Daniels's desk. Dr. Patel's smile widened as he glanced at Linda, his eyes filled with encouragement. "I have some great news for you," he began, his tone warm and reassuring. "Linda, your recovery has been nothing short of remarkable—much faster than we anticipated. Given how well you're doing, I believe you're ready to be discharged from inpatient care."

Linda's heart skipped a beat. She blinked in disbelief, barely processing the words. *Home? Already?*

"You'll continue your therapy as an outpatient," Dr. Patel continued. "Twice a week, you'll come in for sessions to keep building your strength. But you'll be able to sleep in your own bed, be surrounded by your family, and take the next steps toward regaining your independence."

Barbara's eyes widened in surprise. "But patients usually stay here for weeks—sometimes months—don't they?" she asked, her voice laced with both excitement and concern.

Dr. Patel nodded. "That's true, but Linda's determination, along with the incredible support she's had from all of you, has made a world of difference. She's ready."

A mixture of emotions swirled in Linda's chest—relief, joy, and a lingering hint of fear. She glanced at at Barbara, searching her face for reassurance. Could she really do this?

One look at her proud, hopeful expressions, and she knew—yes, she could.

Linda was scheduled to be discharged the following day, her crutches waiting by the door. As she prepared to leave, she couldn't help but think of how far she had come. From being confined to a hospital bed, unable to remember her own name, to standing on her own again. It was nothing short of a miracle.

As they wheeled her out of the Rehabilitation Center, Linda turned to Barbara. "Mom, we're really going home," she said, a radiant smile lighting up her face.

"Yes, sweetheart," Barbara replied, her voice choked with emotion. "You're going home. And this time, for good."

Chapter Twenty-Eight:
Blood Type:
Nancy Talks to the Priest
JJ Talks to the Family

While Linda was improving JJ was impatiently waiting for the blood results from Father Thomas's car. One afternoon while he was going over other ongoing cases the phone rang. It was the State Police Lab

"We have your blood results which I will fax you when we hang up,"

"And?"

"It's human blood and it matches Linda Daniels."

"As I said I will fax you the report with all the details, but there will be no way to dispute this."

"Thank you so much, this is a major help,"!

"I thought you might be pleased to finally close this case."

"He had mixed feelings about the results. It would close the case but he did like Father Thomas."

He pulled out the Lieutenant's card and gave him a call.

"Hi, this is Detective Jason. You can give Brad Huff his keys back. We got the result from the testing."

"Good or bad?"

"It closed the case."

"Congratulations. I'll get someone to drop off the keys this afternoon."

"Thanks so much. I owe you one."

"You can buy me a drink when you're over this way again."

"I will do that."

They hung up. Next, he called Nancy.

He told her the results; said she had good instincts and was glad she encouraged him to follow up on it.

"Can I talk to Father Thomas before you arrest him?" she asked.

"Sure, but why?"

"I'd like to get him to turn himself in."

"Okay.".

. .
.

Nancy found the charge nurse and told her she had to leave for a while. It was an important personal matter, but she could be called or paged if there was an emergency.

She left the hospital and drove to the church. Father Thomas was in his office. When she knocked on the open door he immediately stood and motioned her in.

"It's nice to see you Nancy," he said. "Is there something I can do for you; is there a sick patient in ICU that I should be visiting?"

"No, I've come to talk to you about Linda."

"Did she take a turn for the worse? I thought she was home doing well."

"Oh, Linda is doing fine. She'll have her cast off in a few weeks and be able to bear weight on the injured leg."

"Then what is it?"

"Well, Father, we tracked down your old car. There was blood under it—we had it tested, and it's consistent with Linda's blood type." His face turned ashen, but he didn't say anything. "I'm here to ask you to turn yourself in—spare yourself the embarrassment of being arrested and dragged through a trial."

"I appreciate your concern. You know I spent almost every night with her praying she would recover. If she didn't, I would have turned myself in. But I guess I rationalized that if she did recover, why tell anyone I was at fault? God works in mysterious ways, and he is letting me know now I need to own up to my sins."

"Will you come to the police station with me now?"

"Yes, of course."

"May I use your phone?"

"Certainly?"

Nancy picked up the phone and called JJ, her voice steady but tight with emotion. She told him she was taking the priest to the police station to turn himself in—and that he could now speak with the family.

When she hung up, she turned to the priest, who had already risen and was quietly putting on his coat. Without a word, they stepped out into the fading light, the silence between them heavy with everything that had just been set in motion.

. .
.

JJ took a deep breath as he parked his unmarked police car in front of Linda's family home. He turned off the engine, the silence inside the car growing heavier as he mentally rehearsed what he was about to say. Delivering news like this was never easy, but today, it felt particularly grim. The family he was about to face had already endured so much - Linda's accident, her long stay in the ICU, and her difficult road to recovery. Now, he had to tell them that the very person they had trusted, the priest who had been a source of comfort and support, was responsible for the hit-and-run.

Gathering his thoughts, JJ stepped out of the car and adjusted his jacket, the cool evening breeze doing little to alleviate the knot of tension in his chest. He made his way up the cobblestone path to the front door, hesitating for a moment before knocking. The door swung open, revealing

Brenda, Linda's teenage daughter, her face a mix of surprise and curiosity.

"Detective JJ, good evening," Brenda greeted him politely, stepping aside to let him in.

"Evening, Brenda," JJ responded with a tight smile. "I'm here to speak with your family. Is everyone home?"

"Yes, they're in the living room," Brenda said, leading him down to the living room.

As they entered the living room, JJ was met with the sight of the family gathered together. Tom, sat tensely on the couch next to Barbara, who was holding Linda's hand. Linda was in her wheelchair, her pink cast visible under a soft blanket draped over her legs. The room was filled with an air of cautious optimism as if they were all trying to hold onto whatever peace they had managed to reclaim since Linda's return from the hospital.

"JJ, good to see you," Barbara greeted, her eyes searching his face for a clue about the purpose of his visit. "Is everything alright?"

JJ took a deep breath, steeling himself for what was to come. "I'm afraid I have some difficult news to share," he began, his voice steady but gentle. "It concerns the investigation into Linda's accident."

Tom leaned forward, his brow furrowing, his hands gripping the edge of his chair. "What is it, Detective? Have you found the person responsible?"

JJ let out a measured breath and gave a slow nod. "Yes, we have. Father Thomas came forward earlier today and turned himself in. He admitted to being the driver responsible for the hit-and-run."

The room fell into a stunned silence.

Barbara's face went pale, her fingers tightening around Linda's as if anchoring herself against the sudden, crushing weight of the revelation. Tom's mouth opened, then closed, his mind scrambling for words that refused to come. Linda stared at JJ, her wide eyes filled with confusion, disbelief swirling in their depths.

"Father Thomas?" Linda's voice was barely above a whisper, as if saying his name out loud might somehow make it less real.

JJ gave a solemn nod. "I know this is difficult to hear."

"But... but he's been part of our lives for years," Barbara murmured, her voice trembling. "He baptized Linda. He officiated our wedding. How could he—?"

Tom shot up from his seat, his hands raking through his hair. "No," he said, shaking his head, his voice thick with denial. "There has to be some mistake."

JJ met his gaze, steady and unwavering. "I wish there were."

A heavy silence settled over them, broken only by the distant hum of hospital machinery. The betrayal cut deep, sending a shockwave through their family that none of them had been prepared for.

"Father Thomas?" Barbara whispered, her voice trembling. "How... how could he have done this?"

JJ nodded, understanding the shock they were feeling. "I know this is hard to hear. We wouldn't have believed it either if we didn't have solid evidence. Nancy offered to share a lead with me. I then decided to inspect Father Thomas's car. We found traces of blood on the car, and blood analysis confirmed it was Linda's."

Linda gasped, her hand instinctively reaching for the cast on her leg as if it could somehow protect her from the painful revelation. "He... he just drove away?" she whispered, her voice barely audible.

"Yes," JJ confirmed softly. "He admitted that he panicked. He claims he didn't realize it was you until he heard about the accident. By then, he was too scared to come forward. It's not an excuse, but... it's the truth."

Barbara shook her head, tears brimming in her eyes. "We trusted him. He was like family."

Tom, who had remained silent, finally found his voice. "What will happen to him now, Detective?" he asked, his tone clipped and controlled, betraying the storm of emotions roiling beneath the surface.

"Father Thomas will be charged with reckless driving and leaving the scene of an accident," JJ explained, his voice steady but laced with a hint of regret. "Unfortunately, we don't have enough evidence to charge him with driving under the influence. But he will face time in prison for his actions."

The weight of his words settled over the room like an oppressive fog, thick with disbelief and heartbreak.

Linda was the first to break the silence. Her voice, barely above a whisper, trembled with emotion. "He... he came to see me in the hospital," she said, staring at the bedsheet as if searching for answers in its folds. "He prayed for me... for my recovery..."

Barbara inhaled sharply, her grip on Linda's hand tightening as fresh tears welled in her eyes. "I can't believe he would do this," she murmured, shaking her head. "How could he betray us like this?"

Tom, who had remained silent until now, let out a slow, measured breath. His jaw was clenched, his hands curled into fists at his sides. "A man of God," he muttered, his voice edged with disbelief and quiet fury. "And he left her there... like she was nothing."

No one had an answer. The betrayal ran too deep, the wound too fresh. And as the reality of it all sank in, the pain in the room became almost palpable.

JJ, realizing that there was nothing more he could say to ease their pain, nodded respectfully. "I'm truly sorry for all that you've been through. If you have any other questions, don't hesitate to reach out. I'll take my leave now."

As he turned to go, he paused for a moment. "Please, take care of each other," he added softly before stepping out of the door.

The room was left in a heavy, suffocating silence after he left. Brenda, who had been quietly standing by the door, shifted uncomfortably. Finally, she cleared her throat.

"There's... something I need to say," Brenda said, her voice shaking. All eyes turned toward her. She hesitated, glancing nervously at Tom before continuing. "I... I thought Grandpa was the one who hit Mom. I... I saw him that night."

Tom's face went pale, a bead of sweat forming on his forehead. "What... what are you talking about, Brenda?" he stammered.

Brenda took a deep breath, the words tumbling out in a rush. "I was driving with Steve that night. We saw you, Grandpa. You were swerving on the road, and you looked... drunk."

Barbara's eyes widened in shock, turning toward Tom with an expression of disbelief. "Is this true, Tom? Were you drinking that night?"

Tom hung his head, unable to meet her gaze. "I... I was, Barbara. But I swear, I didn't hit Linda. I was terrified when I found out about her accident. I thought... maybe it was me. Maybe I was the one who did it."

Linda's face flushed with anger and betrayal. "You've been carrying that guilt this whole time? And you never told us? Not even when I was lying in the hospital bed, fighting for my life?"

Tom's eyes brimmed with tears, his throat tightening as he struggled to find the right words. But before he could speak, Barbara's sharp voice sliced through the air like a blade.

"You should have told us, Tom!" she snapped, her face flushed with anger and hurt. "We've been suffering, tormented by the unknown, not knowing who did this to our daughter. And all this time, you let us believe it was a stranger—when deep down, you thought it might have been you?"

Tom flinched as if struck, his shoulders sagging under the crushing weight of guilt.

Linda's fingers trembled as they gripped the armrests of her wheelchair. Her voice, though quiet, carried the heavy weight of exhaustion and disappointment.

"Take me to the room, Mom," she murmured, her gaze fixed downward. "I... I need to be alone."

The only sound that followed them was the faint scrape of Linda's cast. Tom's eyes filled with tears as he tried to speak, but Barbara's sharp voice cut him off. "You should have told us, Tom! We've been suffering, not knowing who did this to our daughter. You let us all think it was a stranger when you thought it might have been you!"

Brenda reached out and placed a hand on his shoulder. "You don't have to lose everything, Grandpa. But you need help. You need to get better - for all of us. For Mom."

Tom nodded slowly, wiping his face with the back of his hand. "I'll quit drinking," he promised, his voice a hoarse whisper. "I'll go to rehab. I'll join AA. I need to fix this... before I lose all of you."

Brenda hugged him tightly, tears finally escaping her own eyes. "We'll help you, Grandpa. But you need to take that first step."

Tom nodded, stepping back and taking a deep breath. "I... I need to clear my head. I'm going for a walk. I'll be back soon."

As he walked out the door, Brenda watched him go, hoping that this time, he would find the strength to keep his promise.

Epilogue

Tom did keep his promise. He went to rehab and then joined Alcoholics Anonymous and remained sober. His sobriety and more involvement with the family helped repair their dysfunction as Linda continued to heal. But deep down inside, he harbored a deep hatred of Father Thomas and what he did to the family while trying to appear caring and helpful.

Father Thomas was fined $5,000, sentenced to six months in prison, and had his license suspended for 180 days upon release. The court had been lenient, considering that he had turned himself in and pleaded guilty to all charges. While serving his sentence, he joined Alcoholics Anonymous, seeking redemption in the quiet corners of his confinement.

Meanwhile, life moved forward. Nancy and JJ continued seeing each other, their bond growing stronger now that the case was behind them. At dinner on their first date after the trial's conclusion, JJ couldn't stop talking about how much he respected her instincts.

"In fact," he admitted between bites of his steak, "you really did solve the case."

Nancy smiled, shaking her head. "No," she countered, meeting his gaze. "It's what you said after we found the bag phone. We make a good team."

Later that evening, JJ walked her to her door. The night air was crisp, but the warmth between them was undeniable. As they stood there, lingering in the moment, he leaned in, and she met him halfway. Their first kiss was soft yet full of promise—a quiet beginning to something new.

Addiction

If you know anyone who has a problem with alcohol or drugs, develop a plan that will meet their needs, whether it is rehab, therapy or meetings that deal with their challenge and offer them assistance.

This is the first chapter of my next book.
THE LAST CONFESSION:
Nancy and JJ

The Prologue

On Sunday the altar boys were getting ready for mass but Father Thomas was nowhere to be found. As the congregation waited for mass to start people began to murmur "What's taking so long?" Finally, an altar boy came to the pulpit and said, "We can't find Father Thomas."

Several men in the congregation got up and followed the altar boy to the sacristy. Then they headed to his living quarters and again no Father Thomas. They called his name and there was no answer. They looked outside and his car was parked in its usual spot. They walked around the church buildings calling his name but there was no response or any sign of him.

They went to find Betty, the part-time secretary and Ralph the custodian but neither of them had seen him since Wednesday.

Ralph said, "I thought it was strange. He usually comes to see me in the morning and to inspect the church, but I figured maybe someone was sick or he had an appointment. Seemed unusual though two days in a row".

At that point, they decided to call the police to file a missing person's report. It took some time to get the police to agree to investigate as he was an adult. Finally, they reached JJ and he immediately drove to the church bringing an officer, Michael, with him.

He asked all the congregants still there to please sit down. He instructed Michael to get the names, addresses and phone numbers of each person after which they could leave.

He talked to Paul who he knew attended AA. He asked him if Father Thomas had been present at the AA meeting on Wednesday.

Paul replied, "The second A in AA is anonymous".

JJ said "I understand that but it is not a secret that he attends AA. He hasn't been seen since Wednesday and now appears to be missing."

Paul answered, "Yes he was at the meeting on Wednesday evening."

"Did he look normal or did anything unusual happen at the meeting?"

"It was a normal meeting. Tom didn't show up so there was less tension as Tom remains angry with Father; he has a hard time with him being there".

Next JJ began searching Father's office and he noticed a speck of blood on the floor. His desk looked a little messy, but otherwise the furniture was in place and it didn't look like there was any disruption. He got his kit and collected a specimen of the blood and sealed and labeled it properly.

Then JJ looked through the desk drawers, at his bookcase and in the closet. Nothing seemed out of place. He headed for his living quarters. The kitchen was spotless. He checked all the cupboards, drawers and even the refrigerator and oven. Again, everything was in order. He moved to the bedroom. The bed was made neatly. He pulled back the covers and found nothing. He looked under the bed, in the drawers of his bureau and in his closet.
Everything was neatly in place. There were papers on his desk which were notes for his Sunday sermon. The room was perfectly normal.

He continued his investigation outside. Father's car was parked in its usual spot. The keys were in the ignition. He searched the car which was impeccably clean and finally opened the trunk which also was clean with a jack, spare tire and nothing else. He walked around the church buildings and saw nothing unusual.

He took notes of everything. He asked Michael to canvas all the houses nearby and get the names and telephone numbers of all the residents at home and the addresses of those that were not home. He then went back to the station to map out a grid search and figure out how to create a way for all the people at church and in the neighborhood to be interviewed.

Father Thomas had completed his jail sentence early for the hit-and-run incident that had shaken the community. Now, news of his sudden disappearance spread like wildfire. It was as though the town couldn't catch its breath. The anger and betrayal that many felt toward him had softened and been replaced by worry and a collective fear that something terrible might have happened.

In his small, cluttered office, Detective Jason or JJ, as everyone called him, was studying a map of the surrounding forest. The lines on his face seemed deeper today, and his normally sharp eyes held a bit of concern. The disappearance wasn't sitting right with him, and the pressure was mounting. He glanced up as Officer Michael, one of the younger members of his team, walked in, holding a notepad and looking equally unsettled.

JJ motioned for him to close the door, then leaned back in his chair. "Michael, I don't like the look of this." His voice was steady.

"Neither do I, sir. Do you think it could be a kidnapping for ransom?" Michael replied, pulling a chair closer to the desk.

JJ exhaled slowly, his gaze drifting to the window. Outside, the golden rays of the late afternoon sun did little to ease the tension in the room. "I hope not," he said after a pause. "But if it is, then at least that means Father Thomas might still be alive."

Michael scribbled a note in his pad. "What's the next move

"We need to cover our bases," JJ replied. "Start with the obvious, we'll need plenty of posters. I want his picture printed and posted on every street corner in this town and beyond. Someone, somewhere, might have seen something. Make sure to include a number for tips."

"Understood."

JJ tapped his pen against the map, his thoughts racing. "While you're handling that, I'll work on organizing a search party. We'll start with the woods. If someone's hiding something or someone, they might think the forest is a good place to keep it hidden. And if the worst has happened…" He trailed off, his jaw tightening.

"I'll get the posters sorted immediately," Michael said quietly, not needing him to finish the sentence. He stood and started toward the door but hesitated. "Do you think this could be connected to the hit-and-run case? Maybe someone seeking revenge

JJ considered the possibility. "It's crossed my mind," he admitted. "But we don't have anything to go on yet. Let's focus on finding him first."

Michael left the room, leaving JJ alone with his thoughts. Running a hand through his hair, JJ stood and grabbed his jacket. If Father Thomas was out there, lost or in danger, JJ was determined to find him. The town had been through enough; it didn't need another tragedy.

He stepped out into the hallway, his mind already ticking through a list of townsfolk who might be willing to join the search party.

. .
.

JJ headed toward the community center, where he had arranged to meet locals interested in volunteering for the search party. As he walked through the streets, he noticed how quiet the town felt. The weight of Father Thomas's disappearance hung heavy in the air.

When JJ arrived, he was surprised to see the room filled with familiar faces. Nearly the entire town had turned up, from shopkeepers to farmers, all eager to help; everyone but Ron Whitlow.

"Alright, folks," JJ began, addressing the crowd. "I appreciate everyone coming out. We're going to need all hands-on deck for this search. The woods are dense and vast, so we'll split into groups and take shifts; morning, afternoon, and night. Each group will cover a designated area and we'll rotate to make sure every inch is swept."

There was a murmur of agreement as people divided themselves into teams. JJ provided maps and assigned each group a section of the forest to search.

. .
.

JJ quickly returned home after the community meeting; his mind still preoccupied with the details of organizing the search. He slipped out of his shoes at the door and let out a long sigh. It had been a long day already, but the evening ahead promised to be just as busy. Yet, before Father Thomas went missing, he had had something to look forward to; a date with Nancy. Now he would have to cancel it.

He dialed Nancy's number and she answered right away,

"I'm guessing you have to cancel our date," she said.

"You are very intuitive."

"So, any progress on finding Father Thomas Nancy asked, her tone shifting to one of genuine concern.

JJ shook his head. "Not yet. We've got search parties heading into the woods this afternoon and I need to meet them at the Community Center to coordinate the search.

"Do you think he might have... you know, gone willingly? Maybe to clear his head or get away from everything JJ considered this for a moment.

"It's possible, but it doesn't explain why he hasn't told anyone. He's not the type to just vanish without a word."

"That's true." Nancy replied, her expression thoughtful. "And if it's something worse... like foul play? What's the town saying?

"The town's in a strange place. Everyone was still coming to terms with what he did to Linda, but now, with him missing, they're praying for his safe return. It's like the anger's been replaced by fear and worry."

"You'll figure it out darling. You always do. Just don't forget to take care of yourself, okay "Thanks, Nancy. I'll try."

· ·
·

The first day of the search was marked by optimism and determination. Volunteers moved through the woods methodically, calling out Father Thomas's name and scanning for any signs of him. JJ moved between groups, ensuring everyone stayed organized and focused.

But as the days stretched and no trace of Father Thomas was found, the enthusiasm began to wane. People grew tired and disheartened. Slowly, volunteers started dropping out, citing exhaustion, work obligations, or the simple belief that the effort was futile.

By the end of the month, the once-dedicated search party had dwindled to nothing. On the last evening, JJ stood at the edge of the woods, watching the last group of volunteers walk away. The forest loomed before him, dark and unyielding, as if guarding its secrets. Tom and a few others continued the search on weekends. But in a month, with all the searchers, they had hardly covered half of the wooded areas.

JJ ran a hand through his hair, frustration bubbling to the surface. He wasn't ready to give up, but without the town's help, his resources were limited. Father Thomas's disappearance was turning into a puzzle with too many missing pieces.

The search might have ended for now, but JJ's determination to solve the puzzle hadn't wavered. He would keep digging, one lead at a time, until the truth was uncovered.